Communist
Revolutionary
Warfare

INDOCHINA BEFORE THE TRUCE OF 1954

COMMUNIST
REVOLUTIONARY
WARFARE

The Vietminh in Indochina

GEORGE K. TANHAM
The RAND Corporation

FREDERICK A. PRAEGER, *Publisher*
New York

BOOKS THAT MATTER

Published in the United States of America in 1961
by Frederick A. Praeger, Inc., Publisher
64 University Place, New York 3, N. Y.

Second printing, 1962

Library of Congress Catalog Card Number: 61-16698

Printed in the United States of America

This book is Number 96 in the series of
Praeger Publications in Russian History and World Communism.

PREFACE

Recent events in Laos and South Vietnam indicate that the Communists are continuing their expansion in Southeast Asia. Although no formal invasions or declarations of war have been made, military actions ranging from ambushes to battalion-size engagements have taken place. Even more important, political indoctrination has been carried on extensively, with a consequent weakening of the authority of the legal governments. Although prediction of future events in this area must necessarily be uncertain, an examination of past Communist activities there should provide certain insights and thereby indicate means of coping with this continuing threat. This study focuses primarily on military aspects of the war and attempts to provide insight by means of an analysis of Vietminh military doctrine, tactics, and organization as revealed during the 1945–54 war in Indochina. Although no attempt has been made to present a narrative history or a description of all aspects of the Vietminh regime, the study clearly reveals the core of Communist revolutionary warfare, namely its emphasis on the integration of all means—political, economic, military, and psychological—to win the war, and, above all, to win the minds of the people.

The Vietminh success in Indochina clearly demonstrates the effectiveness of revolutionary warfare in an underdeveloped area. In both the strategic and tactical areas, it offered the Communists the greatest potential gain at the least possible risk. The initial low level of violence tended to preclude Western intervention, and at the same time involved the least risk of any possible loss of prestige for the Communists. It also enabled the Vietminh to pose as leaders of the insurgent nationalist movement and to gain popular support, while behind the scenes consolidating their power, which led to eventual control. Tactically, guerrilla-type warfare enabled the Vietminh to retain mobility in the difficult jungle terrain, facilitated the gathering of intelligence information, and attrited the French forces, while permitting the Vietminh to build up the regular forces necessary for the formal battles of the final stage of the war. Thus, the major lesson to be learned by the West is that guerrilla operations of the Vietminh type will probably continue to be important, and that nuclear and other modern weapons have by no means rendered obsolete the more "primitive" forms of warfare.

Countries economically underdeveloped, and with strong feelings of resentment and dissatisfaction along with impatient aspirations, provide fertile ground for revolutionary movements. This combination of material needs and ideological poverty makes such countries particularly receptive to Communist aid and ideas.

If the free world is to prevail in the struggle against further Communist expansion and is to assist these countries in their own independent development, it must better understand their needs and the appeal and tactics of the Communists. It is hoped that this case study will assist in meeting the present challenge.

ACKNOWLEDGMENTS

It gives me pleasure to acknowledge the contribution of a number of individuals and organizations without whose help this book could not have been written.

Most of my research was done in Paris, where the French Army was most cooperative in giving me access to their war records and special studies on Indochina. I am indebted to General Cossé-Brissac, Director of the Service Historique de l'Armée; General Larroque, Director of the Centre d'Etudes Asiatiques et Africaines; and to many other French officers who must remain anonymous, for their valuable assistance and many courtesies.

I wish to thank Anne M. Jonas of The RAND Corporation's Social Science Department for the preparation of Chapter VI, as well as for her general assistance and advice. My colleagues, Victor M. Hunt, William W. Kaufmann, Edwin W. Paxson, and Hans Speier, deserve special thanks for their warm encouragement and valuable comments on the manuscript. And without the unstinting and expert editorial assistance of Sibylle Crane, this work might never have been completed.

Above all, I am deeply grateful to the United States Air Force and to The RAND Corporation for supplying the opportunity and the support that made this study possible, and for enabling me to visit Vietnam and thus gain first-hand knowledge of the physical conditions under which the war in Indochina was fought and of the people who fought it.

Most of this book was written as a part of Project RAND, the research program conducted by The RAND Corporation for the U.S. Air Force. Needless to say, the opinions and conclusions expressed herein are entirely my own and do not reflect an official position of either the U.S. Air Force or The RAND Corporation.

GEORGE K. TANHAM

CONTENTS

Communist Revolutionary Warfare

INTRODUCTION

During World War II, an underground resistance movement—the Vietminh—developed in Indochina under the leadership of Ho Chi Minh. Although there can be little doubt today that this movement was largely Communist-inspired and that Ho himself was an old Communist, the spirit of nationalism was predominant at the time, and the revolutionary aspirations of the movement seemed confined to ousting the Japanese rulers. By the end of 1944, the Vietminh had set up a guerrilla high command. But, although supported and supplied by the United States, its relatively small force of poorly equipped guerrilla fighters was quite incapable of taking significant action against the Japanese.

In the spring and summer of 1945, the situation changed. On March 9, 1945, the Japanese disarmed and interned the French troops in Indochina, who until then had remained at liberty there in spite of the Japanese occupation. This act resulted in great loss of French prestige, particularly since it was becoming increasingly evident that the Japanese were losing the war. Thus the stage was set for release of all the forces for independence that had been gathering momentum over the years. Almost immediately the moderate Bao Dai, former Emperor of Annam, proclaimed himself "emperor" of an autonomous Vietnam. And two weeks later, General de Gaulle himself made some vague references to Vietnamese autonomy, thereby adding to nationalist hopes of gaining independence peacefully. Events shattered these hopes.

On August 10, the Vietminh High Command gave orders for a national uprising against the Japanese. Although officially directed only against Japan, the move was also obviously intended to forestall any subsequent return of the French. The revolt was so immediately successful in the north that Bao Dai abdicated his post of self-appointed titular head of the country. Ho Chi Minh formed a provisional government on August 29, and four days later proclaimed complete independence for Vietnam. With the success of this insurrection, the Communist element among Vietnamese nationalists gained a strong hold on the leadership of the revolutionary movement.

The French, although determined to reoccupy Vietnam, were for the moment stymied by their lack of troops and transportation. The Allies, however, came to their aid. In mid-September, British troops occupied the southern half of Indochina, and Chinese Nationalists the northern portion. The population's anti-British sentiment ran so high that the British commander, General Gracey, then found it necessary to proclaim martial law in his area. On September 23, a few French troops arrived at Saigon, seized the public buildings there, and immediately set about reestablishing French authority. Large French reinforcements arrived during October.

Ho Chi Minh realized that he faced a difficult situation and that if he were to succeed, it would be necessary to rally all Vietnamese nationalists to his cause. In an effort to disguise his Communist backing and in order to give his movement a patriotic stamp, he dissolved the Communist Party on November 11 and formed a "national front."

Before attempting the reconquest of the insurgent stronghold in the north, it was first necessary for the French to obtain the withdrawal of the Chinese Nationalists. In February, 1946, the French reached an agreement with Chiang Kai-shek that stipulated that Chinese troops would leave northern Vietnam, in return for which the French would give up all special rights in China. Ho appears to have been sufficiently impressed by this accord to decide that concessions to the French were necessary if he were to avoid the head-on collision for which he was as yet unprepared. At any rate, he agreed to French occupation of certain positions in north and central Vietnam. When French troops entered north Vietnam, they encountered both Chinese opposition and sporadic Vietminh attacks.

Efforts to arrive at a peaceful solution continued. On March 6, 1946, a *modus vivendi* was worked out whereby Ho allowed French troops to enter Haiphong and Hanoi, while France agreed to recognize Vietnam as a "free state." The French, perhaps deliberately, made no attempt to define this term precisely, a failure that later proved to be the germ of very serious difficulties. Neither side ever really accepted the March 6 agreement, and a series of conferences in the spring and summer of 1946 served merely to underline the irreconcilability of the two camps. The only tangible accords (such as the so-called "September agreement," which dealt chiefly with economic and cultural questions) tended to ignore the vital issues.

While the French continued their military reconquest, the Vietminh laid plans for the eventual ouster of all French troops.

On November 23, 1946, after a series of incidents in Haiphong, the French ordered the Vietnamese, under threat of reprisals, to evacuate their section of the city within two hours. Compliance with such an order was clearly impossible, and the French, true to the letter of their ultimatum, bombarded and wiped out the Vietnamese sections of Haiphong that same day.

This event, coupled with the patent inconclusiveness of the year's negotiations, apparently convinced the Vietminh of the hopelessness of this approach, and on December 19, the Vietminh ordered a surprise nationwide attack on all French forces. Though December 19 has become the commonly accepted date for the outbreak of the war, it is clear that intermittent hostilities between French and Vietnamese preceded this date by more than a year.

Throughout the war, Vietnamese independence remained the major political issue. In the earlier phase, the moderates in the nationalist camp were still open to a compromise with the French, under which they might have been ready to accept modified autonomy, had it been coupled with the promise of eventual independence. But the French, in their understandable unwillingness to surrender a prized possession and with shortsighted determination to avoid concessions in the direction of independence, remained blind to the possibility of an alliance against the Communist threat. French failure to support the moderate element thus vitiated an attempt by moderate nationalists, in May, 1947, to establish a "Front of

National Union" in Saigon. By this and other evidence of their intransigence, the French slowly but inevitably alienated even the most conciliatory of the nationalists and drove most of them either into the revolutionary camp or into exile. In September, 1947, the French High Commissioner made a modest move in the right direction by offering "liberty within the French Union" to nationalist leaders, a proposal that was accepted by some of the moderates. Again, however, he failed to specify precisely what this phrase meant in practical terms. Moreover, the irate Vietminh took punitive action against those Vietnamese who had supported the proposal. Still, as late as 1948, the moderate Ngo Dinh Diem proposed to the French that they grant dominion status to Vietnam, a suggestion that was rejected.

In June, 1949, the French, perhaps in growing awareness of their error, invited Bao Dai to head a Vietnamese government, but by then most nationalists had become thoroughly distrustful of French motives, and the Communist Vietminh had clearly attained control over the nationalist movement. Bao Dai had neither popular support nor authority and showed little interest in governmental affairs.

To have underrated the force of nationalist feelings and to have disregarded all opportunities for genuine compromise may be called the basic French mistakes in Indochina. Failing to realize in time the crucial importance of popular support in this type of war, they remained oblivious to the fact that their disregard of popular will helped their enemy to consolidate forces and led thus to the inevitable success of the Vietminh.

I

VIETMINH MILITARY DOCTRINE
AND THE WAR

In 1945, even before the Japanese surrender, Ho Chi Minh began to develop a regular army for the newly constituted Communist Vietminh government. The guerrillas of World War II (who had been trained and supplied mainly by the United States) were enrolled in this army and trained for conventional warfare. The Communist leadership believed that, given some time to build this kind of army, it could afford to wage war on the French, by then generally weakened, and drive them out of the country. Japanese and Allied armaments, though useful, were insufficient for the army's needs; it has been estimated that, in late 1946, Ho's force of 60,000 men had only 40,000 rifles. Nevertheless, on December 19, 1946, Ho suddenly launched attacks on the French forces in Hanoi and other garrison towns throughout the country. The inferiority of the Vietminh forces was very quickly revealed, and by spring 1947, the Vietminh government and the remnants of its army fled to the mountainous area north of Hanoi. A French operation in the fall of 1947 narrowly missed capturing Ho and destroying the remains of his army.

The inability of the Vietminh to achieve a quick victory,

followed by the French failure to annihilate the Communist forces, indicated that a long war was likely. However, the Vietminh recognized this fact far more quickly and more clearly than the French. Consequently, the Vietminh leaders turned to the works of Mao Tse-tung for a theory of war. Their strategic concepts were to be strongly influenced by his ideas, which were singularly well suited to their own struggle. In *Strategic Problems of China's Revolutionary War,* Mao defined as basic to all revolutionary war the four main characteristics of the war in China: (1) a semicolonial country of great size and of uneven political and economic development; (2) the presence of a powerful enemy; (3) a Red Army that started out by being weak as well as small; and (4) a Communist leadership that could rely on popular acceptance of the revolutionary idea, at least in the sense of an agrarian revolution. Whereas factors 2 and 3 pointed to a long war and, Mao warned, might even spell defeat if there were bungling by the revolutionary leadership, factors 1 and 4 strongly favored ultimate success. Starting with these assumptions, which today may appear rather obvious premises, Mao went on to develop his theory of a protracted war in three stages, culminating in victory for the revolution.

In his *On Protracted War,* Mao again started with the specific case of China. While rejecting the idea that China could be subjugated by counterrevolutionary forces, he warned that it would be equally false to believe in a quick and easy victory for the revolution. The war will be long, and will be divisible into three definite stages, whose length cannot be predicted. In the first, given the initial military superiority of the enemy, the revolutionary forces must be on the strategic defensive, while the enemy holds the strategic initiative. During this phase, the Communists must be willing, if necessary, to trade territory, industries, and population for the preservation of their weak military forces. They must be prepared for long retreats, during which they may temporarily grow even weaker. The enemy, however, will also be growing weaker because of lengthening logistic lines, harassment by the Red guerrillas, weakening morale, and increasing unfriendliness of the population. The next stage will begin when the enemy stops his advance and concentrates on holding territory and consolidating his gains. During this second period, as in the first, guerrilla action will be the chief form of warfare, while the regular revolutionary forces are being trained and equipped for the final stage of the war—the counteroffensive, the objective of which will be to annihilate the enemy. In the course of the second phase, the revolutionary forces, though perhaps strategically inferior to the enemy, must gain the tactical numerical superiority that will enable them to win battles. The crucial timing of the counteroffensive will depend not only on the internal situation of the two warring sides but on the international situation as well.

Mao's concept of the protracted war in three stages served as the theoretical basis for the revolutionary war in Indochina. The scope of the present study precludes a detailed comparison of China in 1936 with Indochina after World War II, but it may be helpful to examine the extent to which Mao's four main characteristics of the Chinese situation applied to Indochina.

About one-thirteenth the size of China, Indochina has about one-twentieth its population. Outside the two populous delta regions, there are large, sparsely populated areas which afford shelter for irregular forces and create difficulties for a modern army. A colonial country, unevenly developed both politically and economically, Indochina was initially unable to put into the field a modern army that could stand up to the strong French forces stationed on its soil. Thus, Indochina, like China, provided the opportunity for a strategic defensive and the evolution of the protracted war. However, the Vietminh demonstrated that guerrillas could operate not only in the mountains and thinly populated areas but also in the heavily populated enemy regions, and, indeed, that to some extent it was possible clandestinely to develop a military machine in such areas. While recognizing major dissimilarities between the two countries and certain factors specific to each, one can see the struggle in both wars primarily as one between an underdeveloped regime with limited arms and resources against a more modern power backed by highly developed military forces, though in the case of Indochina the French were 8,000 miles away from their industrial base. However, it is also clear that the Chinese struggle took the form of a civil war among the Chinese, while in Vietnam the war was waged against a foreign power.

Little seems to be known of what Viet leaders were thinking during 1948. The available information indicates that they had accepted the theory of the protracted war and resigned themselves to the fact that they were in the harsh first phase. They confined themselves chiefly to guerrilla warfare throughout the country. Attacks by regular units the following year showed, however, that they had secretly been building regular forces.

Vo Nguyen Giap and the Formulation of Viet Doctrine

For 1949, reports of meetings and speeches by Vietminh leaders permit us to form a more precise idea of the emerging strategy. At a military congress in mid-May, top military leaders expounded the doctrine of the protracted war and stated at which stage they considered the war in Indochina to be. According to Colonel Ly Ban, an officer in the Ministry of National Defense, the military mission of the revolutionary forces would be accomplished in three phases: passive resistance, active resistance and preparation for the counteroffensive, and, finally, the general counteroffensive. Hoang Van Thai, Chief of the General Staff, echoed the same idea. Speaking particularly of the passing from the second to the final phase, he stated his belief that partial offensives should precede the general counteroffensive, and that, before launching the latter, the Vietminh would have to have a tactical force far superior to that of the enemy. Vo Nguyen Giap, Commander in Chief of the Vietminh army, stressed the need to consolidate the principal revolutionary forces. Praising the troops but criticizing the quality of higher officers, he called for improvement in the cadres and the commands and for fullest development of popular support for the regular army. The struggle, he said, was in the second stage, where guerrilla warfare was most important and the war of movement of secondary value. Yet he thought that there ought to be progressively more and larger offensive actions in preparation for the general counteroffensive, and insisted that, before one could afford to pass into the final stage, the war of movement would have to become equal in importance to guerrilla action.

As Colonel Ly Ban pointed out, World War II had shown that guerrillas alone could not win wars, and therefore a war of movement became a necessity. The war of movement, as Vietminh leaders conceived it, was characterized chiefly by the absence of fixed fronts and rear areas, quick concentration for action, and immediate disengagement after fighting. In a seeming paradox, although the Vietminh always spoke of a war of movement and of the importance of avoiding pitched battles, the war was essentially one of attrition, in the sense that all efforts, military and nonmilitary, were aimed at wearing down the French. This was particularly true of the first two phases of the war, when the enemy was being weakened for the *coup de grâce* of the third stage. But an essential part of this over-all strategy of attrition was the multitude of tactical operations, as well as the decisive offensive of the third phase, all of which were based on movement and mobility.

The outstanding military figure of the Vietminh was Vo Nguyen Giap. Born in 1912, he became a Communist at an early age and was a veteran of French jails before World War II. His anti-French feelings were further intensified when the French police, he claimed, killed his wife and sister-in-law. Giap studied revolutionary tactics in China, gained experience in organizing guerrillas in

World War II, and became head of the Vietminh guerrilla command in 1944. A former history teacher and
holder of an advanced degree, he urged his troops to study
and reflect on their own combat experiences so as to improve themselves continuously.

Moreover, Giap took his own advice, and the fruit of his
reflections and self-critique was a book, published in 1950,
entitled *La guerre de la libération et l'armée populaire*
(*The War of Liberation and the Popular Army*), which
to this day remains the fullest expression of Vietminh
doctrine. While accepting Mao's concept of a three-phase
war, Giap felt uncertain about the possibility of drawing
clear divisions between the several stages. This uncer-
tainty may have arisen from his awareness of the unique
situation of Indochina, with her two major theaters of
operations—the southern area around the Mekong Delta
and the northern one around the Red River (or Tonkin)
Delta. Progress in the two areas had been quite different
and was to continue so to the end of the war. In the north,
the Vietminh in 1945–46 built up a regular army, which
took the field against the French but was quickly defeated.
Nothing like this happened in the south. By the end of the
war, the north was entering phase three, while the south
had hardly emerged from phase one. Only in the northern
theater of operations, therefore, can the development of
the three phases be traced fairly clearly.

Giap claimed that the failure of the French to defeat the
Vietminh in the north in 1946–47 had marked the end of
any hope for a short war and, he implied, had allowed the
factors determining a protracted war to come into play.

To understand Giap's critique of Vietminh strategy, one

must recall the developments of the early war period. During the first phase of the revolution, which began in the south (Cochinchina and South Annam) in 1945, the Vietminh took the strategic defensive. In the north, on the other hand, various agreements with the French accorded Ho's government *de facto* recognition, and the uneasy peace lasted until the surprise Vietminh attack of December, 1946. By these agreements, the Vietminh gained time in which to prepare their military forces and to win popular support. In their propaganda campaign, they could point to these accords as indications of their own love of peace, and when it became expedient to break them, they argued that it was in fact the French who had broken them and so precipitated the war. The failure of the attacks of 1946–47 forced the Viets into the defensive in the north also and ushered in the first phase of the protracted war. After the regular forces had been beaten and their remnants compelled to disguise themselves as civilians or to seek shelter in the area northwest of Hanoi, the war continued clandestinely. While the Viets were sacrificing—carefully, however—territory, people, and economic assets in order to preserve a hard core, they never relaxed their efforts to win over the population. The activities of clandestine cells, guerrillas, and propaganda agents proved increasingly damaging to the French, and slowly the Vietminh gained the loyalty of many of the people. Ho and Giap clearly had accepted Mao's precepts regarding the importance of preserving the cadres and winning popular support.

Although Giap never mentions the disastrous attacks of December, 1946, in his book, he obviously found profitable lessons in the Viet failures of this early period. In the first place, he saw that a sound strategy alone was not enough; good tactics also were a necessity. Among the tactical mistakes, he included poorly conceived ambushes, efforts to hold certain terrain too long, and attempts at encirclement of the enemy after he had received strong reinforcements. In this connection, Giap noted the dangers conventional warfare held for weak forces: "For an army relatively feeble and poorly equipped, the classical concept of war is extremely dangerous and ought to be resolutely rejected." He pointed out that the greatest failures had come about when the Vietminh had departed from guerrilla tactics and attempted formal battles. Failure in the south, he believed, was due to inadequate political guidance for the troops and ineffective training, while in the north it was attributable more to improper military training and insufficient understanding of the true nature of guerrilla warfare. Lastly, Giap thought that it had been a strategic mistake not to regard Indochina as a single theater and, consequently, that the neglect of Cambodia and Laos had been a basic error in the conduct of the war. (In this respect, the writer believes that Giap was mistaken: Geographically, racially, and historically, Indochina was not homogeneous, and the subsequent attempts to make it into one strategic area failed.)

According to Giap, the second phase of the war had begun in 1947, and at the time of his writing (in 1950) was still in effect.* The intervening years had been favor-

---

* Most observers would place the beginning of phase two in 1949, as the French retained the initiative during 1947–49 and the first Vietminh attacks of a formal nature did not occur until 1949.

able to the Vietminh, both in their own revolutionary achievements and in the developments that were taking place in the French camp. The Vietminh had continued their strategy of defense and had built up the size and quality of their forces. He wrote:

> The activities of the independent companies conducted at the same time as those of the armed propaganda teams, the guerrilla units, and the village militia were the principal forms of combat used to advance our guerrilla war, to destroy enemy reserves, and to protect our own reserves. Since popular "bases" were indispensable to the development of the guerrilla war, we dispersed the companies of each battalion and we permitted them the necessary liberty of action so that they could infiltrate different regions and cement their friendly relations with the local populace. Since the companies were relatively weak, they had no difficulty in understanding the necessity for firm popular bases. Thanks to their intimate acquaintance with the different regions, they easily won the support of the local population. Their close connection with popular bases gave a strong impetus to the armed conflict. When the guerrilla units acquired enough experience, when the local militia became powerful enough, the dispersed elements of the companies in the different localities gradually regrouped themselves.

The winter of 1949–50, in particular, was described by Giap as a period of visible progress for the Vietminh. The rate of preparation increased, offensive actions became more frequent and daring, and small units were developing into larger line units. There was increased emphasis on the regular forces and the war of movement. The regional and communal forces, however, were not neglected, and guerrilla warfare was, if anything, intensified.[*] He summarized the effort as follows: "We must work without stopping to improve the conditions of our forces, to attrite the enemy forces, to make the balance gradually tip in our favor in order to proceed rapidly toward the third phase."

Giap believed that the French at this time had turned primarily to defensive warfare and had reduced their goals in Indochina. To some extent this was true. Although the French continued to carry out clearing operations and limited offensives in the late forties, they never again came so close to complete victory as they had been in 1947. They had considerable success with pacification efforts in the south, and the Vietminh leaders admitted this fact. However, Giap clearly recognized the weaknesses of the French situation. He predicted that, as the war wore on, the French would have to use colonial troops and even Vietnamese,[†] that they would never have adequate manpower or supplies, and that their morale would decline.

Both Giap and Ho Chi Minh regarded 1950 as the decisive year, and intimated that phase three was not far off. According to Giap, the three requirements for passage to

---

[*] For a more detailed discussion of the distinguishing characteristics of the regular army, the regional troops, and the popular forces, and of their relationship to one another, see pp. 41–47.

[†] It should be remembered that French law prohibited the use of French conscripts outside France; hence the full burden of the war fell on the French regular army and the Foreign Legion.

the third phase were superiority of the revolutionary forces, a favorable world situation, and a noticeable weakening of the enemy. He wrote: "We will not move into a general counteroffensive until our strength in all areas [political, economic, and military] is reflected in our military strength." In 1950, the Vietminh army was approaching in number that of the French and was developing the capability to concentrate and maneuver in major campaigns. Many French troops were increasingly tied to forts and bases, permitting the Vietminh to attain tactical superiority more easily. The arrival of Chinese forces at the border, in December, 1949, presaged outside aid. The military capability of the French, on the other hand, was suffering increasingly from lack of reinforcements, from dispersion, and from logistic difficulties; the French clearly were on the defensive, and their will to fight was weakening. Perhaps most important, French procrastination over Vietnamese independence had alienated more and more of the population.

Giap's optimism in 1950, however, was still qualified by several reservations. For one thing, he considered the French military forces still superior to his own battle corps because they possessed a more effective command system, more and better equipment, and greater firepower. Furthermore, he confessed that the execution of the war of movement, which alone could bring victory, had proved more complicated than he had foreseen. A shortage of staff officers and specialists made the solution of command, communications, and logistic problems unexpectedly difficult. Lastly, and quite significantly, he indirectly admitted that there were still large segments of the population that had not been won over to the Vietminh cause and hence would not provide a secure base for regular-army operations.*

Giap's view of phase three, which he described as the stage of "the general counteroffensive," whose primary objectives were to annihilate the enemy and reconquer the national territory, was not as simple as Mao's. The name was given not because it implied an attack on all fronts, but because it led to final victory. He conceived of this phase as having several subdivisions, only in the last of which would there be formal battles. Before progressing to the third phase, the Vietminh would have to be certain of (1) the absolute moral superiority of the revolutionary forces; (2) a considerable improvement in the material position of their army that would narrow the French economic advantage (Giap described the agricultural economy of Indochina as ideal for guerrilla actions but less so for larger, more formal operations); (3) an international situation more and more favorable to the Communists; and (4) a strong and purposeful direction of the war by the Communist leadership, in contrast to less and less sure command by the enemy. In all four respects, he thought, the Vietminh would benefit greatly by the widening disagreements between the French and the Americans and by the political divisions within France.

All forms of warfare were to be employed during stage three, but the war of movement would become more and more important, while guerrilla warfare would assume

---

* It is true that more and more of the people were alienated by the French, but they did not therefore all rally enthusiastically to the Vietminh cause. Even those, however, who merely became indifferent thereby created difficulties for the French and thus indirectly aided the Vietminh.

secondary value. There would also be an increasing number of formal engagements. The war of movement, in Giap's opinion, was best suited to the Communist forces, for it not only took advantage of their superior morale but allowed them to corner and annihilate the enemy. Guerrilla warfare, however, would always remain important because it, too, depended on high morale and, moreover, was less handicapped by inferiority in matériel. Furthermore, in the final phase, the irregular forces would be a major link in the logistic system of the regular army.

Giap contended that the final phase might be long or short and that its duration could not be entirely controlled by the Vietminh, though they could influence it. The absolute moral superiority of the Vietminh might make the phase short because:

> This will enable us to accelerate our pace, aided by the willing sacrifice of the population, their resistance and revolt in regions occupied by the enemy, and because of the increase in our forces due to general mobilization and help from abroad. This superiority could bring about great reverses to the enemy: dislocation of rebel troops, growth of antiwar sentiment among French troops. The French domestic situation could be severely affected by defeats in Indochina, by pacifism, and by independence movements in the colonies. Grave errors might be made by the French in their strategy.

On the other hand, the material poverty of the Vietminh, continued French resistance in the south, and more active

American and British intervention could prolong the phase. If this were the case, the war would take on the more classic form of warfare, with pitched battles and long campaigns.

THE USE OF MAO'S THEORY

While Mao's theory of the protracted war provided an outline for the conduct of the revolutionary war in Indochina, several principles of his were stressed in Vietminh doctrine. One of these was the "security of the rear." This term did not mean to the Vietminh what it does to Western military persons. In Western terminology, it is a way of saying that provisions have been made by the military forces to assure the functioning of the rear echelons without enemy interference. To the Vietminh, "security of the rear" meant that the people of the country had been won over to the revolutionary cause and that wherever the army operated, it would receive warm support. The army depended on the population to form a secure base for its operations. Once the people had been indoctrinated, it was not enough for them merely to be sympathetic to the cause. The regular army relied on them for such positive contributions as food, shelter, intelligence, and transport. When necessary, the local inhabitants also provided hiding places for the troops, and often accepted them into their midst for long periods of time.

Popular support alone, however, did not govern the choice of areas of operation. There are indications that such other circumstances as terrain and enemy initiative, and especially the combination of these two factors, may have been even stronger determinants. Because of French concentration in the Red River Delta, the Vietminh were forced to remain and operate chiefly in the mountainous areas outside the Delta, where the various minorities were not particularly sympathetic. These people believed the Vietminh to be a Vietnamese movement, and as they had always disliked the Vietnamese, they now distrusted the Vietminh. The Vietnamese, on the other hand, who were the most sympathetic to the Vietminh cause, lived in the Delta and coastal regions, where the Vietminh could not operate freely.

The principle of the security of the rear—in reverse, as it were—governed the Vietminh's efforts to create insecurity in enemy-held areas. To this end, guerrilla groups were organized in the French areas, which very effectively not only harassed the French military forces, but politically indoctrinated the population and undermined the French regime and, later, the French-sponsored national Vietnamese government. These Communist cells waged propaganda war and established shadow governments in the villages and sometimes even in larger administrative units. Certain Vietminh adherents (known as *Dich Van*) even attached themselves to the French forces in order to defect as soon as their leaders ordered them to do so.

The importance of the guerrilla fighter in the Vietminh theory of war can hardly be exaggerated. Active in all phases of the war, he was effective in constructive as well as destructive ways. Whereas the Soviets had considered the guerrilla a useful auxiliary to the Red Army, the Vietminh used him in many more ways and proved that he could operate anywhere. Aside from their obvious tasks of sabotaging, harassing, ambushing, and attacking the enemy, the Viet guerrillas waged political warfare in both friendly and enemy areas. Often they provided some of the screening and security forces for the regular army; they also "prepared the battlefield" (which involved stockpiling, intelligence-gathering, and sometimes fortification), and fought against the French clearing operations. On many occasions, they were called upon for logistic help. The Vietminh experience showed, furthermore, that guerrillas could be developed even in urban areas, as, for example, in the French-held outskirts of Saigon. As will be shown later, Giap also infiltrated regular units into the thickly populated Tonkin Delta, where they acted as guerrillas.

Again following the Chinese lead, the Vietminh formed "bases" that served several purposes. In Viet definition, the characteristics of a base area are "a closely integrated complex of villages prepared for defense; a politically indoctrinated population in which even children have their specific intelligence tasks; a network of food and weapons dumps; an administrative machine parallel to that of the legal authority, to which may be added at will any regular [army] unit assigned to operations in the area." The typical base thus was equipped to serve as a nucleus for Vietminh government and a strongpoint for military operations. These organizations might be clandestine or open, depending on the situation. The most important of the early base areas was northwest of Hanoi.

Mao had recognized the difficulty of selecting the right moment for launching the general counteroffensive, and the Chinese had had considerable arguments over this question of timing. The Vietminh experienced similar difficulties and differences of opinion. Giap, while fully accepting Mao's doctrine of the protracted war, seemed impatient to pass into phase three. Although his own analysis of the situation in 1950 had revealed his reservations about the Vietminh capability at that time, he pressed for going into the offensive during the first months of that year. He was opposed by the head of the Communist Party, who argued that conditions were not yet favorable for phase three. Just how widely this issue was discussed is not known, but the military congress of 1950 approved Giap's plans.

During the last half of 1949, the French had shifted their primary field of operations from Cochinchina in the south to Tonkin in the north. The most important reason for this move was the arrival of Chinese Communist forces at the Indochina border. Furthermore, the French were concerned over the growing strength of the Vietminh in the north, and felt that the success of pacification in the south rendered this transfer of the main effort possible and safe. There were dangers involved, however, as the shift of large numbers of troops to the northern area detracted from the clearing operations and the maintenance of the *status quo* in the south.

The north having become the most important theater of operations, Giap struck at the string of French forts on the Chinese frontier in the autumn of 1950, and, in the famous battle of Route Coloniale 4, nearly annihilated the French garrisons. Giap himself appeared surprised by the extent of his victory and was slow to follow up his success. According to many observers, Giap's forces, despite this successful action, were not ready for open battle because the regular army was not yet fully formed. This contention seems to be borne out by the subsequent limited defeats inflicted on Giap by French forces under Marshal de Lattre at Vinh Yen (January, 1951) and Mao Khé (March, 1951), and by the partial defeat at the Day River (May, 1951). After these reverses, Giap withdrew his forces at the end of the fighting season and set about recruiting, equipping, and training a stronger army.

Marshal de Lattre, who took command in Indochina in December, 1950, not only followed but improved on the tactics of his predecessor, General Carpentier. Carpentier had established a system of posts and forts to protect the Tonkin Delta and to provide a secure base, relying on mobile units for offensive operations. The marshal regrouped his troops and organized mobile groups to act as his striking forces and to provide mobile reserves. These measures required a great number of men, and consequently some outposts were relinquished and certain areas voluntarily surrendered to the Vietminh. But, whereas De Lattre apparently had been trying to create a secure base from which to strike out offensively, his successors, after his death early in 1952, became more and more tied to the defensive functions of this system. Also, De Lattre had been singularly able to inspire his troops; succeeding commanders, on the other hand, were increasingly faced with morale problems.

In November, 1951, the French struck at and captured Hoa Binh, thereby severing the north-south communications route of the Vietminh. Giap counterattacked, but the French had anticipated his move and indeed had planned to attrite his forces in a set battle. Giap suffered heavy casualties but continued the battle for three months, engaging in a protracted campaign of position warfare that was contrary to Mao's ideas.* Faced with increasing supply problems, heavy losses, and Vietminh infiltration of the Delta, the French reluctantly abandoned Hoa Binh. They deprecated the seriousness of this withdrawal by claiming that they had by then accomplished their objective of forcing Giap into pitched battles, with resulting heavy casualties.

The Time of Self-Appraisal

In August, 1952, at the seventh anniversary celebration of the Vietminh revolution that had led to the establishment of the People's Republic, the Vietminh leaders admitted some of their mistakes in the intervening years; clearly aware of the setbacks of 1951, they forecast a long war. As Vice President Pham Van Dong put it, "Resistance is in the seventh year of its existence. It still will last a long time and many difficulties remain to be surmounted." Truong Chinh stressed the need for guerrilla activity, and even Giap said that the Vietminh "must energetically pursue the fight in the enemy's rear." All the speakers agreed on the need to wear down the French still further and to conquer the rural masses politically. The tenor of the speeches was far more guarded and less

---

* The French, by striking at one of the enemy's more weakly held key points, may have taught Giap a trick he was later to use against them.

optimistic than had been the case in 1949–50; it was evident that the Vietminh had underestimated the enemy and miscalculated the timing of the counteroffensive (though Ho still spoke of it as "coming in the near future").

Even during this period of rebuilding and self-examination, however, Giap apparently felt compelled to continue the offensive. Possibly, he believed the situation to be ripe and attributed his earlier failures to improper tactics. But it is equally possible that he had a correct estimate of the situation but found more compelling reasons for staying on the offensive, which, in view of the 1951 defeats, meant abandoning the precepts of Mao. Although we cannot be sure what his motivations were, scattered evidence points to the important conclusion that, for once, there were serious morale problems in the Vietminh camp in general and in the army in particular. Success in the autumn of 1950 may have raised hopes that made the defeats of the following spring all the more disappointing. Some peasant unrest had been created by the Vietminh land reforms and changed fiscal policies. According to the French, Ho had never really captured the peasant support in the way Mao had in China, and his supporters among the peasants were adventurers and malcontents. While the French charge is obviously exaggerated, there is little doubt that Viet leaders had some problems of morale in the army and among the peasantry at this time.

Giap now reverted to operational tactics that avoided pitched battles and attempted instead to draw the French out of their strong points in the Delta. This strategy of *zones excentriques*, as the French called it, was rather similar to Liddell Hart's "indirect approach." Giap decided to strike in areas that, although lightly held, had certain political and psychological value to the French and called for at least a token defense. The obvious choice for such operations were those mountain areas where certain ethnic minorities had remained sympathetic to the French. The invasion of the Thai° country, in September, 1952, was an excellent example of this strategy, and it worked exactly as Giap had planned it. Except for the single tactical mistake of staging a prolonged attack on one of the French strongholds, the operation was brought off expertly.

As the French forces were concentrated in the Red River Delta, the mountainous regions were weakly held, but for obvious reasons the French were reluctant to evacuate them. They were thus faced with the dilemma of having either to abandon these mountain people or to dispatch forces from the Delta, thereby weakening the Delta defenses. Even if they chose the latter alternative, they could not afford to send out forces adequate to cope with Giap's main force in these difficult areas, for to do so would have been to leave the Delta open to massive infiltration. In the end, the French avoided making what may indeed have been an impossible choice, and tried, instead, to follow both courses. As a result, they were unable to muster sufficient strength in either area; the forces they sent into the mountains proved inadequate there, but their absence seriously weakened the Delta

° Part of Indochina, not Thailand.

defenses. The defeat at Dien Bien Phu was in large part the result of a similar error in French strategy.

In the autumn of 1953, the French concluded a treaty with Laos that provided for membership of this mountain kingdom in the French Union under conditions very satisfactory to the French. The possibility of a Vietminh invasion of Laos, however, aroused French concern, and, in November, General Navarre decided to occupy Dien Bien Phu in order to force Giap to cope with this stronghold before invading Laos. Navarre also hoped to create such a strong camp that the Viet attack would be not only unsuccessful but costly. Thus, the occupation of Dien Bien Phu was to serve the dual purpose of protecting Laos and forcing the Viets to attack a strongly held position to their own detriment.

The announcement, in January, that an Allied conference was to convene at Geneva the following April to deal with the problem of Indochina apparently influenced the Vietminh to make an all-out effort against Dien Bien Phu—even to the point of accepting a siegelike battle and heavy casualties—for the sake of political gains at Geneva. Giap now recalled the 308th Division, which was even then engaged in the invasion of Laos that the French had meant to forestall, and put it around Dien Bien Phu.

April 26 marked the opening of the Geneva Conference and the beginning of the final, bloody assault on Dien Bien Phu. Slowly but surely, Vietminh superiority of numbers and firepower ground down the French position. On May 8, the garrison surrendered, and the Vietminh had won a tremendous political victory.

This battle, while violating one of the major tenets of

Viet doctrine (namely, that pitched battles, and particularly sieges, must be avoided), confirmed certain others. First and foremost, it demonstrated the importance of subordinating military considerations to political ends. Though the battle of Dien Bien Phu clearly hurt Giap's battle corps (the French estimated that he lost 15,000 men), the political advantages and the blow to French morale in Indochina, and particularly in France, far outweighed these losses. The experience of Dien Bien Phu also revealed the virtue of the Vietminh's painstaking preparation for battle, their skill and diligence in camouflage and digging in. It is hard to determine whether the use of direct artillery fire, which may have been decisive, was forced on the Viets by their crews' lack of training in the conventional use of artillery, or whether it was deliberately chosen as most appropriate for the terrain.

In a strictly military sense, the defeat at Dien Bien Phu was not necessarily catastrophic for the French. Giap had suffered heavily. Furthermore, the French garrison, while important enough, accounted for only one-fifteenth of the total number of French troops in Indochina. But the political repercussions, as foreseen by the Viet leaders, were such that Paris decided to end the struggle.

II

THE VIETMINH MILITARY
ORGANIZATION

The twofold objective of the Vietminh military organization was to create ideological uniformity throughout the country and to develop an efficient modern army. To these ends, the Communist leadership set out to develop a military machine with strict political controls, centralized authority, and uniform territorial organization. Almost from the beginning, the military forces were divided into three groups of varying combat capabilities: the regular army, the regional forces, and the popular troops. Furthermore, the Communist Party maintained a political organization within the army that paralleled the military at all echelons. These were the few basic organizational characteristics that remained unchanged throughout the war. For the rest, the Vietminh's dedication to the Communist principle that organization should not be static but should reflect progress, and their acceptance of Mao's theory of the protracted war in three stages, meant that the military establishment had to be in a constant state of organizational evolution. The need for practical experimentation under atypical war conditions further contributed to this state of flux. In the course of time, small guerrilla groups grew into modern divisions, which in turn underwent modifications. The simple guerrilla command of 1944, after numerous changes, became the complex general staff of 1954. The political organization within the army, cautious and limited in its powers of control during the first years of struggle, ultimately developed into a highly influential organism.

In the last years of the war, the National Military Council, composed of President Ho and the ministers of Defense, Interior, and Finance, directed the over-all war effort. Responsibility for the military conduct of the war lay with the Ministry of National Defense, whose internal organization, too, was altered as old problems were solved and new ones arose.

Early in the war, the Vietminh shared high government positions with leaders of nationalist groups. But gradually, as they perfected their Party organization, developed Communist leaders at the lower echelons, and gained greater popular support, they began to ease non-Communists out of responsible positions. Certainly, by the early 1950's, the Viets had won a tight hold on the military apparatus and were pursuing Communist ends in addition to their nationalist objectives.

At the time of the cease-fire, the Ministry of National Defense was headed by Vo Nguyen Giap. As Commander in Chief of the army, Giap had operational control as well as administrative responsibilities. The ministry was organized on the Chinese pattern, with three major subdivisions: the Political Bureau, the General Directorate of Supplies and Maintenance, and the General Staff.

THE POLITICAL BUREAU

The Vietminh regime, like any other Communist government, attached enormous 'importance to the political aspects of war. A political organization within the military establishment was designed to assure proper ideological indoctrination of the soldiers and the integration of military actions with political objectives. In the early years of the war, when co-operation with national groups was policy, the power of the political agents (commissars) was still limited; military commanders had the final decision on military issues, while the activities of the political officers were restricted to purely political matters. As the Vietminh element in the government became more powerful, however, the balance shifted. By 1950, there were instructions on the books stating that, in case of a conflict between the military commander and the political commissar, the latter's view was decisive. (The Russian experience, however, may lead one to overestimate the role of the commissars. In Indochina, as in China, the military leaders were themselves Communists, who had fought long and hard for the movement, were generally loyal to its goals, and thus required relatively little political supervision.)

By the end of the war, the Political Bureau had been established within the Ministry of Defense as the highest organ for political control in the armed forces. Both the territorial commands and the divisions had what were called "Delegated Political Commissars." Even in temporary commands, such as the "fronts,"* political officers maintained close supervision over all activities. In the higher units, these men would be assisted by various committees. At the division level, for instance, there were committees for administration, political instruction, recreation, preparation of the battlefield, propaganda for civilians, propaganda against the enemy, and the affairs of the Party. At lower levels, the organization became simpler. No political commissars existed below the company level, but in every platoon a political cell worked closely with the company political officer. At company level, there was a political organization called the Military Council, composed of men who were elected by the members of the company for a three-month term but were subject to recall. This council was a "democratic" device, whose alleged purpose was "to educate the troops and provide political guidance, not to allow the men to argue or dispute with the officers." When the company was divided, the various platoons had their individual, smaller military councils.

Parallel to the official political organization within the army, there apparently was a clandestine Party organization, which at certain levels merged with the political organization. Every company and battalion had its Communist cell, with a subcell for each company section, and a secretary who was responsible for the work and discipline of both cell and subcell. If the cell had more than nine members, it elected a smaller group, called the Committee of Delegates, to work with the secretary as

* See pp. 39–40.

an executive committee. At regimental and at division level, the Party organization merged with the political organization in the Subcommittee for Party Affairs under the political commissar.

While Party organization men, by definition, were members of the Communist Party, this was usually, but not necessarily, true of officials in the political organization. The political officers wore uniforms and were members of the armed forces, but they enjoyed a privileged position.

THE GENERAL DIRECTORATE OF SUPPLIES AND MAINTENANCE

The second major subdivision of the Defense Ministry, the General Directorate of Supplies and Maintenance, had four bureaus: food, clothing, and equipment; armament and ammunition; health; and transport. These services were nowhere as complex as their modern Western equivalents. Before the emergence of the regular army, the supply system was largely decentralized; only with formation of the battle corps and the advent of massive Chinese aid did it become more centralized and complex. Little is known about its organization, but the operation of the logistic system will be discussed more fully in the chapter following.

THE HIGH COMMAND AND GENERAL STAFF

The Vietminh High Command, from its inception, had a wide variety of responsibilities, some of them not normally those of a high command. In the beginning, one of its major functions was that of guerrilla command. (Although there was a so-called General Staff, it was very rudimentary in form.) In April, 1947, the Supreme Command, as it was then called, had five major subdivisions: an Intelligence Service, a Political Service, a Bureau for Popular Troops, an Inspector General, and a General Staff. The General Staff was very simple in its organization and was concerned with operations, which at that time consisted mainly of small but numerous guerrilla actions. Its other major function, in the early stage of the war, was the training and organization of larger units, with the ultimate objective of forming a modern field army. Operations and training remained the General Staff's primary missions until late 1949 or early 1950, when planning, in the Western sense of the word, began to play a much larger role in the work of the High Command.

In 1950, a more modern General Staff, based largely on the French model, was created or, more precisely, reorganized from the older one. The cabinet of this new General Staff had four sections: local security, communications, accounts, and administration. The four major staff officers were in charge of personnel, intelligence, operations, and supply, much as is the case in the American army. Under the General Staff were the territorial commands and the line outfits (then regiments). The organizational pattern made it apparent that the staff was intended to plan and direct the operations of large units. Its strongest point was probably intelligence, its weakest, supply. Also, Giap lacked sufficient numbers of trained staff officers, and many of the weaknesses of his organization were a reflection of this shortage.

THE GENERAL STAFF AFTER 1953

By 1953, the staff organization had become still more elaborate, and the changes clearly reflected Chinese influence. The four familiar staff divisions had been dropped and replaced by the more numerous Chinese "bureaus." Vietminh officers were being trained in Chinese schools, and a large group of Chinese advisers was attached to the Viet army, especially to the General Staff. The latter now had ten bureaus, in keeping with its growth and the widening scope of its activities. The two most important were the Political Bureau of the Staff, listed first on the organizational charts, and the Directorate of Operations. Working closely with these two, but organizationally under them, was the Bureau of Important Affairs, in charge of training and planning for at least six months ahead.

As the Vietminh developed divisions and began to anticipate operations of larger scope, they had to plan much further ahead, not only for the usual military reasons, but because of several factors peculiar to the situation in Indochina. One of these was the phenomenon of the "front," temporary headquarters specially established for individual operations involving units of the battle corps. Every front required a certain amount of time to make its plans and to become operational. These fronts must not, however, be confused with those in Western terminology. A Vietminh front was created for a precise tactical mission in a clearly defined area of action, and placed under a commander who was given the means to do the job, including both regular units and such regional and popular troops in the zone of action as were capable of doing auxiliary work and giving logistic help. After the operation, the front was usually disbanded. The Vietminh also attached great importance to what they called "preparing the battlefield," that is to say, to the time-consuming task of assembling stockpiles, gathering intelligence, and sometimes building fortifications. Lastly, they were fond of paperwork: Many French officers have remarked on the incredible number of copies of messages, orders, and instructions that were issued. For all these reasons, the Vietminh needed even more time than might have been expected for the planning of large campaigns. Only for small, regiment-size operations were they able to plan and act very quickly, and even then the effective use of surprise often made it appear as though they had moved faster than they in fact had.

The remaining seven bureaus of the General Staff of 1953 consisted of directorates for Intelligence, Training, Administration, Armed Forces, Popular Troops, Military Affairs, and Communications and Liaison. In addition, there were a special Engineer and Artillery Section (suggesting the expected arrival of engineering equipment and artillery in ever greater amounts), and a Code Bureau. The main supply and maintenance functions had been taken away from the General Staff and, after the Chinese example, had been placed under a separate organization. The new staff was superior in training and experience to the General Staff of 1950. It was able to control the actions of several divisions, and proved that it could plan and execute operations of the size and scope of Dien Bien Phu.

The High Command now assumed the role of field army headquarters and staff as well as that of the highest military planning unit. It combined the functions of air force headquarters, air staff, a training command, and numbered air forces (or, in American army terms, the duties of the general staff, Continental Army Command, and field armies). As the regular army remained relatively small (about the size of a U.S. field army), this combination of tasks was not so difficult as it might seem at first glance. Furthermore, shortages of trained personnel probably rendered this concentration of direction and responsibility essential.

THE REGULAR UNITS

Directly under the High Command, in its capacity as field army headquarters, were the regular units of the army. Until 1950, the largest unit had been the regiment, sometimes reinforced and called a "group." The rate of development from there on was such that, even without Chinese aid, line divisions would soon have been created. However, the substantial Chinese aid that began coming in during 1950 assured better equipment and speeded the formation of larger units. Toward the end of the war, there were six divisions and several regiments in North Annam.

The first Vietminh divisions (in 1950) were good-size units of approximately 15,000 men. They appear to have had a very high proportion of combat soldiers classified as assault troops and firepower troops, and to have contained relatively small command and service elements. But the organizational charts are somewhat misleading, for, as will be shown below, the combat units included extraordinarily large numbers of supply soldiers.

Almost immediately, however, the Vietminh began to reduce the size of the division quite significantly, from about 15,000 men in 1950 to about 9,500 in 1953. Ostensibly, these smaller divisions were better for the war of movement, but one suspects that another reason may have compelled these reductions: After the costly battles of 1951 and early 1952, the Vietminh may actually have been short of men who were well enough trained to be in the front-line divisions.

Savings in manpower—some real and some illusory— were brought about by organizational changes and certain other factors. The early artillery units showed an unbelievably high ratio of men to weapons; for instance, a heavy-mortar (120-mm.) company, equipped with two pieces, had about 200 men! Though the weapon weighed only about 600 pounds, there were 80 porters per weapon. Again, a 75-mm.–artillery battalion armed with four pieces had nearly 1,100 men, of whom half were porters. The arrival of trucks was the biggest step toward solving the ammunition-supply problem, though to a limited degree the reductions in manpower may be attributed to improved training of the men. Another apparent reduction in the size of infantry divisions was the result of removing their artillery units and concentrating them in one heavy division. And finally, wherever possible, civilian labor was used to replace soldiers.

Over 90 per cent of the personnel of the new, lighter division were members of its three regiments, leaving only about 1,000 men to be distributed over headquarters, the engineers, the liaison service, and the headquarters guards. By Western standards, therefore, the division was not capable of sustained combat. True, the lack of motor transport and other modern equipment reduced the need for service troops, just as the habit of living off the country reduced personal-supply needs. But despite the fact that these shortcomings were hidden assets, the Vietminh apparently believed that all considerations were outweighed by the advantages of having a modern army, which they continued to try to build.

The first heavy division (the 351st), formed in 1953, though its subordinate units had existed for some time, is believed to have had two artillery regiments, one engineer regiment, some transportation elements, and probably antiaircraft units. The independent regiments were largely assault troops, but most of them had recoilless weapons and mortars. Separate AA units, armed with 20-mm. and 40-mm. guns, did not appear until the last months of the war. There were no tank units, although some soldiers had received armored training in Chinese schools. Some special units (e.g., radio intercept) existed as early as 1950, but, in general, the Vietminh were weak in this field.

THE REGIONAL TROOPS

The High Command, in addition to its control of the regular army, exercised command over the territorial military organizations, with their regional and popular forces. The fullest and most efficient territorial organizations were those of North Annam and Tonkin, the strongholds of the Vietminh. They were set up as follows: The highest territorial unit was the interzone, which, in theory, included several zones. In practice, there were certain independent zones directly under the High Command, and some interzones without subordinate zones. Below the interzones or zones came the provinces, which were composed of several districts. At the base of the organization were the intervillages (several villages combined for administrative purposes) and the villages.

The Executive and Resistance Committee, sometimes called just Committee of Resistance, directed the over-all war effort of interzone or zone. It dealt not only with the political, economic, and military aspects of the war but also with local problems of health and culture. One of its members was at the same time the military commander of the interzone and thus took orders from both the High Command and the Committee of Resistance. The local direction of military activities for the area lay with a command committee, composed of the interzone commander, his political counselor, and his adjutant, who were assisted by a staff. The commander and his committee were responsible for recruiting and supply functions; they were in charge of all the regional troops and any detached regular units in their area, and supervised the subordinate territorial commands.

The provincial command, under its own Committee of Resistance, was somewhat less elaborate than the interzone organization and commanded the subordinate district units as well as the provincial battalion. It was composed of a command section supported by a simple staff, with an office for operations and training, one for communications, and an intelligence section. This committee also had some logistic responsibilities.

The district, in turn, had its own Committee of Resistance, which was expected to raise a company of regional troops. Though similar in organization to that of the province, it was even less complex. A command committee consisted of the commander, his deputy, and a Party representative. "Technical cells" reported to the Committee on military intelligence, special espionage, political affairs, propaganda, arms production, communications, and administration. But as the districts were often inefficiently run or poorly organized, the province tended to assume greater powers than would appear from the theoretical organization.

THE POPULAR TROOPS

At the lowest echelon of the military organization was the village, with its individual fighters or small units of popular troops. The importance of these irregular troops should not be minimized; they were the backbone of the Vietminh military organization, as reflected in the very existence of a Directorate of Popular Troops at the ministry level, and of Committees on Popular Troops at the province and district levels. The Vietminh's effort to organize the entire population for the war effort was realized in the villages. The so-called popular troops consisted of two groups: the *Dan Quan*, composed of persons of both sexes and all ages who performed auxiliary military duties, and the *Dan Quan du Kich*, made up of men between the ages of eighteen and forty-five who were part-time guerrillas. The latter were organized into groups of from eight to fifteen men, who elected their leaders and were very lightly armed. In the strong areas, some villages had several such groups, which were combined into sections. There were also the *Dan Công*, civilian porters for the regular units.

The village and intervillage command was headed by a committee of three or four members (usually, though not always, including a Party representative for each village), and a secretary who tended to dominate the committee's affairs. The group directed the defense of the village and the day-to-day activities of the guerrillas. Very active villages often had a small supply of weapons and guerrilla material.

The foregoing description, as was pointed out above, applied chiefly to North Annam and Tonkin. In the south and in Laos and Cambodia, the territorial organization was less fully developed and far less effective. In 1947, the Vietminh established a regular command for the south under Nguyen Binh and virtually ignored Laos and Cambodia. But the long line of communications to the south and the apathetic or frankly unsympathetic attitude of much of the southern population made the task of the commander difficult, and the separate command was abolished in 1952. Nguyen Binh, whom the French described as an able leader, had personal ambitions and apparently tried to engage in large-scale warfare before he had developed a popular base. The circumstances surrounding his death in 1950 remain somewhat obscure, but it is generally believed that he was liquidated. Toward the end of the war, the Vietminh had developed some military organization in Laos, but there was still very little in Cambodia. In general, outside North Annam and Tonkin, their organization lacked continuity, cohesion, and efficiency.

REORGANIZATION

The distinctions among the three echelons of the military forces—the regular army, the regional troops, and the popular forces—were based on differences in training and equipment as well as of mission. It might be said that the three parts of this organization reflected the theory of the protracted war, with the popular forces representing the first period of guerrilla action, the regional forces paralleling the second stage, and the regular army dominating the third and final phase. And just as dividing lines between the stages of the war were sometimes indistinct, so also were the differences among these forces, especially those between the regular and the regional units.

Although the regular army was considered the ultimate weapon for victory, each of the three forces had an essential function to fulfill. As Giap stated, "We must concentrate the regular forces *and increase* the regional forces, or we shall make a false step." The regular army, or *chu luc*, was a precious unit, with a specific and crucial mission. Until 1950, this force, then still in its formative stage, was carefully husbanded, and it rarely engaged in combat when the issue was in doubt. In many of their operations, therefore, the French were unable to make contact with the regular forces but met instead the regional troops. By and large, the regular army was kept free to engage in the war of movement and to select both the field and the time for battle. Inasmuch as it was an elite unit and, of the three forces, had the best equipment, weapons, and uniforms as well as the highest pay, it was held strictly to its primary mission. Such duties as building fortifications and preparing the battlefield fell to the other two forces.

Slowly, and for the most part patiently, the Vietminh built up the infantry into a first-class force. After the precipitous engagements of early 1947 that ended in total defeat, they immediately began to reorganize and rebuild their battle corps, increasing both the number of units and the size and number of weapons in each.

An examination of Regiment 9, one of their best units but not an isolated case, shows the progress and growth that followed reorganization. In 1948, this regiment had six battalions, with a total of 1,800 men; it was equipped with only two mortars and two 75's, plus a few rapid-fire weapons. Three years later, it had only three battalions but 3,500 men, and possessed twenty-four mortars, nine recoilless cannon, eighteen machine guns, and over sixty rapid-fire weapons.

The following figures on regular and regional battalions show the Vietminh's over-all military development in the three main regions between April, 1949, and June, 1951:

The Growth of Vietminh Regular Units

	April, 1949		June, 1951	
	Regular	Regional	Regular	Regional
Tonkin	20	50	78	6
Annam	7	43	21	6
Cochinchina	5	44	18	25
TOTALS	32	137	117	37

These figures reveal a striking increase in the number of regular units in all three areas, and a decline in the regional battalions that was particularly marked in Tonkin and Annam. Although there were almost as many units in the south as in the north, those in the south were smaller and of inferior quality. The steady expansion of the regular forces reflected in these figures may help one to understand why early 1951 could have appeared to Giap as the opportune moment at which to try his battle corps against the French in open battle—an attempt that caused him very heavy losses. The chart can be read, moreover, as reflecting the policy of taking regional forces into the regular army by unit without always replacing them. This development seems in curious contradiction to Giap's own fear that failure to increase the regional units might cause one to "make a false step." It might have been less serious in 1954, when the French were clearly on the defensive in the north and the need for regional troops consequently was less urgent. But in 1951, especially in the light of Giap's own statement, it can hardly have been a matter of preferred policy for the Vietminh. The only explanation that suggests itself, therefore, is that they were not free to choose, but were suffering from a shortage of men with whom to replace those advanced from regional to regular units.

The regional troops were less well organized, trained, and equipped than the regular forces. For the most part, the largest unit was the battalion, though in the latter stages of the war a few of the interzones had regiments. The men in the battalions and companies of regional troops were graduates of the popular forces, who had come in with the limited training that membership in the popular forces afforded. After further training in the regional troops, they advanced to the regular forces, individually or by unit—ideally when they were ready for it, but sometimes only because they were badly needed there. After the arrival of substantial Chinese aid, many of the units had uniforms and more equipment than before, but in general they continued to lack heavy weapons and equipment.

One of the primary duties of the regional forces was to protect an area and its population. They were the troops that met the French clearing operations, launched small attacks, and generally harassed the enemy; in short, they were the "mature guerrillas," who kept the enemy off balance and ambushed his reinforcements.

Their responsibilities extended both upward and downward in the total military organization. On the one hand, they trained and assisted the popular troops. On the other, they were what might be called the guardians of the regular army. Not only did they constitute a reserve and supply reinforcements to the regular forces when needed, but they prevented interference in the army's training and planning, prepared the battlefield for impending operations, protected the regular forces in retreat and advance, and took over some of their defensive missions.

The popular troops were divided into the two groups already mentioned: the *Dan Quan*, which theoretically included almost everyone, and the *Du Kich*, a smaller group that undertook guerrilla actions. The members of both groups served in their spare time, without interrupting their civilian tasks. The *Dan Quan* were essentially a labor force with a tinge of military training. Though occasionally they performed sabotage, their main responsibility was to collect intelligence, serve as guards, make road repairs, build bases, fortify the villages, and—very important—act as porters. They wore no uniforms and had virtually no weapons, except for some sabotage materials. The more selective *Du Kich* had some arms and undertook guerrilla actions on a small scale. They received rudimentary military training and were expected eventually to become line soldiers. Though generally forbidden to assemble in large groups, they were called together in emergencies when it was essential to prevent French clearing operations or to intensify guerrilla activity. Sometimes a few *Du Kich* were infiltrated into enemy-held villages, in order to prepare the way for a Vietminh assault.

But, important as the labor and guerrilla activities of the popular troops were, the Vietminh attributed still greater significance to their ideological mission. The major purpose of these troops was to lend the ideological war of the Vietminh the aspect of a national struggle in which the entire populace participated. The popular forces were also used to recruit young peasants for the military service of the Vietminh.

While apparently quite satisfied with the evolution and performance of the regular forces, Vietminh leaders seem to have felt less happy about the functioning of the territorial organization. At Party congresses and in messages to subordinate organizations, they frequently complained about the inefficiency and mistakes of the lower commands. Among other things, the lower echelons were said to change personnel too frequently: Men were assigned to different units every few months, with detriment to the stability and efficiency of the organization. Another charge was that interzone and provincial headquarters favored the technical cells over the combat units. The High Command admitted the importance of technical groups but insisted that they not be overemphasized at the expense of the fighting units. And finally, the territorial commands were constantly urged to make more efficient use of the population.

In 1952, Ho expressed some of the same misgivings in a severe lecture on the shortcomings of the Vietminh organization in general. The people, he said, were anxious and ready to serve, but they had not been used in the most rational and efficient manner. Furthermore, while noting the progress that had been made, Ho blamed the leaders for bureaucratic excesses and for the increase in waste and corruption (familiar charges in any Communist regime). Some of the cadres, he warned, were not sincerely practicing the principles of the Party and were retarding progress, and a few local leaders who nourished personal ambitions and deviationist tendencies would have to reform or be removed.

Aside from these defects in leadership and organization, the Vietminh had to grapple with certain inevitable problems inherent in the situation in Indochina, which made the formation and efficient operation of organizations difficult. As in any underdeveloped area, there was a shortage of trained personnel, technicians as well as administrators. For lack of lower-echelon administrators, the central administration tended to keep much of the power in its own hands and to issue incredibly detailed instructions to the lower levels. Not only did this severely curtail the initiative of lower officials, but it also put a great burden of time and labor on the top people. As time went on, however, the Vietminh succeeded in training new personnel and thus eliminating some of the worst bottlenecks.

Another serious obstacle to Viet progress was created by the minority groups, most of whom lived in the mountain areas. As mentioned earlier, these groups regarded the Vietminh as a Vietnamese government, and thus as one to be feared and distrusted. Though Giap had succeeded in overcoming some of these prejudices when he worked in the mountainous areas during World War II, he continued to meet a certain amount of opposition all through the revolutionary war. However, the French were slow to exploit their advantage in this respect. It was not until 1953 that they organized guerrilla groups in the mountains to strike at the Vietminh lines of communications. By that time, their dilatory tactics over the granting of independence and their inability to protect the minorities had lost them much of the latter's support.

Another difficulty for the Vietminh lay with the nationalists who were not Communists, yet whose support was essential if the war was to be won. Therefore, even as the Communists became stronger, they were careful to disguise or soft-pedal their purely Communist objectives and to emphasize nationalist and reform ideas to the general population. As late as 1952, when they clearly had control of the movement, they were still cautious about preaching pure Communism outside their own organization.

The Vietminh ultimately perfected an organization that allowed them to defeat the French, and they must be given their due for organizational achievement. Yet there were flaws in the operation of the system, and the speeches of Ho and others testify to the presence of internal difficulties. In dealing with many of these problems, the Vietminh were aided by the inertia and inflexibility of the French. There were opposition groups, for example, whom the French, had they been alert to the situation, might well have used effectively to weaken the Vietminh. Also, if the French had been quicker to recognize the tremendous surge of nationalism and the opportunity it afforded them to meet the demand for independence in good faith, they could have increased the difficulties of the Vietminh many times. Even as late as 1950, many Vietnamese were willing to give the French a chance to show that they meant to stand by their statements in favor of independence for Vietnam, but the French continued to procrastinate. Vietnamese nationalists were thus slowly discredited and forced into the Vietminh camp. It was similar with the potentially strong opposition of the minorities in the mountain areas. Here again, French procrastination, lack of understanding of the needs of these groups, and evidence, now and then, of French duplicity eventually turned those minorities to the Vietminh. With this failure to exploit all opportunities for undermining the Viet organization and movement through political and psychological action, the prospects of a French military victory became more and more remote.

III

PERSONNEL AND LOGISTICS

Few regimes have emphasized as strongly as the Vietminh the importance of the total mobilization of the populace. The constitution of 1946 provided for universal military conscription, and in 1949 the government actually ordered the draft. In practice, however, it did not prove feasible, for the Vietminh government was far from having the bureaucratic machinery necessary to put such a law into effect. Recruiting for the Vietminh army, therefore, remained informal. By the end of the war, Vietminh forces numbered about 300,000 men, a small percentage of the estimated 28 million total population of Vietnam. It is true that the Vietminh controlled the less populous sections of the country; but, on the other hand, they were able to draw many of their recruits from French-held areas.

RECRUITMENT

Since no attempt at conscription was really ever made, the Vietminh have always claimed that the men who served had volunteered. In fact, the Vietminh put great effort into sporadic recruiting campaigns, which combined pressure with propaganda and enticement. It is known that some young men were forcibly dragged into the armed forces, and that in other cases indirect pressure was brought to bear on families or village leaders to supply recruits. Usually, strong-arm and other pressure methods were accompanied by propaganda appeals to the prospective recruits to serve their country against the European imperialists and for the betterment of society. Openly Communistic appeals were generally avoided. Inducements for those who joined included the promise of improved living conditions and a general education. Deserters and prisoners of war were accepted after careful political indoctrination, but their number always remained small.

The motives of the men freely joining the armed forces of the Vietminh were probably often mixed and cannot be determined accurately. Certainly patriotism and, in some cases, Communist beliefs were the dominant motivations. In other instances, the attraction of good food and clothing and possible future education may have been the incentives. The lure of adventure and escape from a dreary life probably caused some to join. A French poll of Viet prisoners of war attempted to discover why they had joined the army. In this group, 38 per cent stated that they believed in the Vietminh cause; 25 per cent expressed resentment at having been forced into the army against their wishes; 23 per cent indicated that they, too, had been compelled to join, but did not seem to resent the use of force; finally, 6 per cent had felt the army provided an interesting career. The survey results should be judged with reservations, because those captured probably constituted the least reliable and most poorly indoctrinated of the army and hence were not a fully representative segment. Periodically, the Vietminh seemed to suffer shortages of man-power—an indication that their means of compulsion and persuasion were not wholly successful. (Women volunteers made up only a small minority of the army's total strength.)

Through their prisoners, the French also sought to discover the social composition of the Vietminh forces. The results of the inquiry showed that 46 per cent of the army was composed of peasants and laborers, with laborers in the majority. (It is not clear why the French did not classify these two groups separately.) According to the prisoners, 48 per cent were petty officials, and the remaining 6 per cent came from miscellaneous professions and trades. If this breakdown is correct, the petty officials provided nearly half the recruits for the army, although peasants made up the majority of the total population. These percentages are especially interesting, as the French controlled most of the urban areas where the largest number of petty officials were likely to reside. They suggest that these officials were more attracted by Communist propaganda than were the peasants, who were also exposed to the pressure tactics of the Vietminh.

Recruiting began at the village level. The Viets attempted to organize the people of every village and group of villages into part-time semimilitarized workers for the Vietminh war effort. Although these people were neither in uniform nor actually part of the military forces, they were potential soldiers. Once they had been politically indoctrinated and had received some very rudimentary discipline, they graduated to the village guerrilla cell and from there to the regional forces.

TRAINING

Training varied not only in the three types of forces, but with the different echelons in each. The popular forces, or guerrillas, had a self-training program, with assistance from the regional troops and occasional aid from noncoms and officers of the regular army. Their training was largely political, but it included some instruction in the use of personal weapons, as well as lessons in sabotage. Some of the more advanced village units had close-order drill and even instruction on automatic weapons. At the district level, companies underwent additional training, with continued emphasis on individual arms, more instruction in the use of automatic weapons, and elementary education in small-unit tactics.

The members of the regional units usually were graduates of the popular forces and thus had had some of the training outlined above. Once they joined the regional forces, they received more individual instruction and began to study unit tactics. Regular army officers assigned to the regional units provided the formal training. In addition, "regional schools" instructed soldiers in the use of the more difficult weapons and in special skills and lower-level staff duties. During this phase of training, the individual not only gained considerable military knowledge but had the opportunity to experience combat and to learn to adapt himself to military life. From these regional troops were eventually chosen the members of the regular army. The process of rising through this system often took several years.

Up to this point, the irregular fighter's training had been sporadic and had in most cases suffered from a lack of weapons and a shortage of instructors. But as soon as he graduated to the regular army, he was exposed to formal and intensive discipline under highly trained Vietminh officers and often Chinese instructors. Moreover, he received a uniform, individual weapons, and better food and equipment.

Upon entering the regular army, the soldier was obliged to take a ten-point oath, in which he swore (1) to sacrifice everything for the good of the cause; (2) to obey his officers completely; (3) to fight resolutely and without complaint; (4) to train diligently; (5) to keep secrets; (6) to bear torture if captured; (7) never to reveal information; (8) to take care of his equipment; (9) to respect and help the civilian population; and (10) to maintain high morale. The oath was not only the soldier's guide as to what was expected of him, but also an indication of the Vietminh's chief points of concern. The fact that two of the ten points dealt with security or the preservation of the "secret" reveals that even the sternly indoctrinated Vietminh soldiers, like men in other armies, could not resist the temptation to tell what their unit was going to do. Morale seemed to be another special concern, and the wording of point 9 underlined the close association of the soldier with the civilian population.

Beyond the requirement of the oath, reminders of the virtues and qualities of the Viet soldier were part of the men's training. A captured document—*The Popular Army of Vietnam*—which originated with the Office of Propaganda and Instruction, contains a lesson-by-lesson outline of a typical indoctrination course. It lists such obvious prerequisites as bravery, patriotism, and the willing acceptance of military discipline, and further demands of every soldier an endeavor to serve the people, to acquire the proper political ideas, and to improve himself in all ways. In addition, the manual calls on each man to have feeling and affection for his fellow soldiers, and literally concludes with the statement: "The army is one great happy family."

Vietminh leaders always maintained that their soldiers fought willingly and happily. In practice, despite their condemnation of discipline in the enemy army, the Vietminh themselves insisted on very strict discipline. But as the above-mentioned manual explained, whereas discipline was tyrannical in the imperialist armies, it was good and proper in the Vietminh army. Communist discipline, according to the pamphlet, was self-imposed, and assured the proper political indoctrination of the soldiers and thus the efficient functioning of the liberation forces.

Since the Vietminh considered infantry the decisive arm of combat, all soldiers received at least basic infantry training. Close-order drill developed precision and quick response to orders; instruction on such personal infantry weapons as rifle, grenade, and bayonet followed. Great emphasis was placed on camouflage and personal protection, and a considerable amount of time was spent on terrain studies and methods of geographic orientation.

Some soldiers were trained as assault troops and were strictly riflemen; others were slated to become members of the firepower or support elements and were, therefore, concerned with heavier weapons, i.e., machine guns, bazookas, recoilless rifles, and mortars. Careful and intensive training was provided on these weapons, and the Vietminh soldier developed great skill in their use, particularly in the handling of recoilless rifles and mortars, which, particularly in the early stages of the war, took the place of artillery.

Once the soldier had become competent with weapons and familiar with small-unit tactics, he was taught larger-unit tactics and the intricacies of maneuvering with heavy-weapon support. Battalion and regimental assault tactics were rehearsed over and over, often with models of French posts and forts simulating the objectives, until the soldier knew his role so well that it had become practically automatic. Actually, however, unit tactics never became as rigid as this might indicate but were adapted to specific situations.

A small portion of the soldiers' time was devoted to obtaining a general education. Many of the recruits were illiterate, and the army provided their first basic schooling and even offered some courses in literature and philosophy.

In the course of the war, the Vietminh developed an extensive school system, partly in Vietnam and partly in Red China. There were schools for the various weapons, and two schools—at Ha Giang and Bac Kan—trained officers for regimental duty. Even before the Red Chinese reached the border, some men had been trained in the Communist-held areas of China, and a few had been trained by the Chinese Nationalists. However, as the Vietminh began to form regiments and to think in terms of division-size forces, their training needs grew. Red China provided schools for noncommissioned, company-grade, and staff officers. Particularly welcomed by the Vietminh were the schools for specialists, who were desperately needed for the more modern army that was being formed: Engineers were trained at the engineers' school at Nanning, while tank troops studied at the armored school at Wu Ming, both in China. Reportedly, some men went to China for pilot training, although the Vietminh never had an air force. It has been estimated that, by the time of the cease-fire, in 1954, up to 40,000 Vietminh soldiers had received training in Red China. In addition to providing school facilities, the Chinese also sent a large number of instructors to Indochina for duty with the staff and regular units and, in some cases, with the territorial commands.

The most important aspect of the soldiers' training, however, and that which consumed the most time, was the political. Its two objectives were to produce politically reliable and enthusiastic soldiers and to provide effective propaganda agents. (Giap stated repeatedly that the soldier's work as a political agent was at least equal in importance to his duty as a fighter.) The opportunities for agents were varied and many, since regular units frequently lived among the people and infiltrated enemy-held areas. The custom of assigning regular army men to duty with the regional and popular forces also furnished wide opportunity for indoctrination.

The aforementioned manual on *The Popular Army of Vietnam* tells a good deal about the nature of the soldiers' political indoctrination and reveals the themes that were stressed most heavily. It begins with a brief history of the army, to which, significantly, it refers as the "troops of propaganda and liberation." This thought is restated in the definition of the army's two principal missions as being, first, to spread propaganda in order to win people to the cause and to gain recruits, and, second, to wage the armed struggle against the enemy. The main arguments of the pamphlet are that the French have deprived the Vietnamese of their independence as well as their individual liberties, and that the tyranny of imperialism must be smashed. There are only subtle and minor references to Communist aims, though the Communist Workers' Party (*Dang Lao Dong*) is praised for its effective leadership.

A favorite Communist device—self-criticism—was widely used in political training. Captured Vietminh material is full of such self-critiques, painstakingly written by semi-literate soldiers who had been forced to look back into their lives and to confess any crimes they might have committed against society. These reports went into considerable detail and covered all facets of life. One young soldier, for example, admitted that he had stolen some rice at the age of six and had, in later years, been selfish in his dealings with other members of the village. The moral was always that one must be willing to sacrifice oneself for the welfare of society.

The large amount of time and careful planning devoted to political indoctrination brought results. There is no question that the Vietminh were able to create a large and dedicated army. Desertions were very rare, and morale problems relatively few.°

° One major exception was the period of low morale after the Vietminh defeats early in 1951. See p. 29.

MEDICAL SERVICES

In this underdeveloped country there naturally were few doctors, and certainly not enough to answer the needs of the armed forces. However, the Vietminh attempted to provide medical service for their regular units. Their goal was an ambitious one: About half a mile from the battlefield there was to be a collection point where all the wounded men would be assembled and given a cursory examination. At a sorting area, about three to six miles from the front, doctors would separate the more seriously wounded from the slightly injured and evacuate them to a hospital some five to ten miles farther to the rear. (The hopeless cases would not be moved and would be left to die.) Approximately twelve to twenty miles from the front, there was to be an operating hospital. In practice, nothing like this existed. However, every regular division had a medical company, usually with at least one doctor, and maintained an evacuation and hospital service. In several of the Viet-held areas there were recuperation points. By the time of the cease-fire, the Chinese had sent large amounts of medical supplies to Indochina, but they had not been able to train the necessary medical personnel, or spare enough of their own, to supply the Vietminh with an adequate, well-functioning organization. Medical service for the regional and popular forces was virtually nonexistent and at best very primitive.

COMMUNICATIONS AND LOGISTICS

There is little precise information on the Vietminh communication system. Viet leaders were quick to recognize the importance of communications, and early in the war tried to purchase radios from foreign countries and to repair captured or abandoned Japanese equipment. At the beginning, before the advent of massive Chinese aid, the great diversity of equipment complicated the repair and maintenance problems, particularly in view of the shortage of trained technicians. The Vietminh did succeed in repairing the civilian telephone and telegraph lines of the country and using them for routine messages. But while they employed the civilian radio net, they were anxious to develop their own military network as far as possible. By the end of the war, thanks to Chinese aid, even units as small as companies and platoons had at least one radio and were thus in communication with their adjacent units and higher headquarters. Semaphore units were used at times, and messengers remained a very important element of the communication system. There was also an elaborate system of runners with relay stations.

Throughout the war, on the other hand, the Vietminh was troubled by the various phases of logistics—the production, acquisition, and transportation of arms, food, and equipment. They had started out with some Japanese equipment, part of it stolen and the rest freely given at the time of the Japanese surrender. Some matériel had also been parachuted to them by the Allies during the fight against the Japanese. Early in the war, a considerable amount of equipment was shipped from Thailand to the Vietminh, but in 1948, a change in Thai foreign policy closed off this supply. Nationalist China sent aid by land and sea (even though the French ostensibly had control of the sea),* and some matériel came from the Philippines. With the exception of what had been acquired from Japan, most of the equipment was of American make. Other matériel was captured or stolen from the French in the course of the war. Indeed, the Vietminh set up a price scale for such stolen equipment, by which they were willing to pay up to three hectares of national land for certain special items.

Local production was a major source of arms and equipment. Many small shops, employing from ten to fifteen workers, would operate in a given area. Partly or wholly mobile, they could be moved from place to place according to the threat of the French advance. These shops made the crudest sort of equipment, with manpower often the only source of energy and automobile motors and simple engines available only at times. Some workshops limited themselves to making mines and explosives, which were used heavily by the guerrillas. Production in these workshops was geared to local needs, and even at the end of the war, there were few factories producing for nationwide

---

* As recalled in the Introduction, the Chinese Nationalists, after the Japanese surrender in World War II, agreed with the Allies to occupy northern Vietnam, ostensibly to hold that territory until the French were able to return to Indochina. Actually, however, the Chinese were not unwilling to help the Vietminh. They had designs on the harbor of Haiphong, important to Chinese commerce, and indeed had hopes of replacing the French, or at least of retaining control of the Tonkin area. Hence they played the Vietminh off against the French.

consumption. A notable exception was the manufacture of bazookas, which was centered entirely in the Tonkin area. The larger shops and factories (employing up to 500 persons) were more or less permanently located in firmly held Vietminh bases.

There were few factories in the south, though small and dispersed shops existed in the Plaine des Joncs, Cochinchina. Cambodia also had some important shops near Ampil, but Laos had virtually none.

Despite the shortage of precision tools, power, and raw materials, the Vietminh managed to produce fairly large quantities of materials. In the first six months of 1948, for instance, the Viets reported that shops in one intersector produced 38,000 grenades, 30,000 rifle cartridges, 8,000 cartridges for light machine guns, 60 rounds for a bazooka, and 100 mines. Another sector produced 61 light machine guns, 4 submachine guns, 20 automatic pistols, and 7,000 cartridges in the entire year 1948. Besides manufacturing, some of these shops excelled in repairing and modifying weapons. None of them, of course, was able to produce any heavy equipment, though one factory in Tonkin was making 120-mm. mortars as early as 1949.

Only with the arrival of Chinese aid did the logistical problems of the Vietminh begin to be solved. According to reliable estimates, petroleum products and munitions comprised 75 per cent of Chinese aid, while the remaining 25 per cent consisted of arms and medical and signal equipment. Though the precise extent of Chinese aid is not known, the following figures seem to be generally accepted: In 1951, the rate of aid from China was about 10 to 20 tons per month. By the end of 1952, the flow had risen to 250 tons, and in 1953, it averaged between 400 and 600 tons. At the beginning of the assault on Dien Bien Phu, Chinese aid was said to be up to 1,500 tons a month, and by June, 1954, it reportedly had reached 4,000 tons.

It has been estimated that 75 per cent of Chinese supplies entered Indochina at Ta Lung and went by way of Cao Bang, Nguyen Binh, Bac Kan, and Thai Nguyen to Vietminh in the west or around the French-held Delta to forces in the south. A secondary route led from Pinghsiang in China to Dong Dang, Lang Son, and from there by poorer roads to Thai Nguyen. Two other entrance points, Lao Kay and Ban Nam Cuong, were considered of little importance. The Chinese had built a railroad to the Indochina border in the east, but there was none to take the goods from the border into Indochina. Materials, therefore, had to be stored whenever the Viet transport schedule fell behind, particularly after supply routes had been hard hit by air attack.

In this underdeveloped country, with its one or two railways and few roads, transportation was bound always to pose a problem, and to the very end of the war, the coolies were its mainstay. The Vietminh organized what they called the "auxiliary service," which was essentially a labor force of local inhabitants. It provided transportation facilities by coolies and whatever equipment was available. In an attempt to control this organization closely, the Vietminh allowed only certain units or headquarters—such as the General Staff, the General Directorate of Food, interzone commands, and other high echelons—to call on its services. The auxiliary force was organized in groups of 15 men each, with 3 groups making up a section and 3 sections a company. With this simple organization, the Vietminh accomplished almost incredible logistical feats.

Logistics experts had drawn up tables showing what could be expected from this primitive transportation system. For instance, on the plains or on reasonably level land with few obstacles, the coolies were expected to do 15.5 miles per day (12.4 at night) carrying 55 lbs. of rice or from 33 to 44 lbs. of arms. In mountainous areas, the day's march was shortened to about 9 miles, or 7.5 miles at night, and the load was reduced to 28.6 lbs. of rice and 22 to 33 lbs. of arms. It was estimated that buffalo carts could carry approximately 770 lbs. and travel about 7.5 miles per day, while a horse cart could carry only 473 lbs. but could travel about 12.4 miles a day. The Vietminh made important use of mule companies, and also of bicycles, which were loaded with as much as 150 pounds and pushed by coolies. Wherever possible, they also took advantage of the waterways.

After the Chinese Communists had reached the border, the Vietminh slowly built up their motor transport, and it was estimated that by 1953, they had a total of close to 1,000 trucks. About a third of these were organized into Regiment 16. This unit, whose task it was to carry supplies from the border to the main depots, was divided into 9 companies, each with 90 to 100 men and approximately 35 trucks. The 9 companies operated independently of one another, rather than in the motor-pool fashion of the American army. This was dictated by the fact that the French air force, in its attempts to interdict the supply system, had succeeded in cutting a number of bridges, and the Vietminh did not have the engineers to repair these bridges rapidly enough, so that the area of supply and communication had been cut into a number of segments. The Vietminh simply put a truck company of Regiment 16 into each of these segments, which thereupon became a self-sufficient transportation sector, with its own gasoline stocks, supplies, and repair shops. Though this system involved innumerable transfers of equipment, the plentiful supply of manpower enabled it to operate successfully.

As the need arose for new roads or supplementary routes, the Vietminh marshaled the necessary labor force and constructed them. Thus, in the late fall of 1953, a road was built from Tuan Giao to a point near Dien Bien Phu to assure the delivery of supplies for the impending battle.

While this primitive use of manpower yielded results, it caused a serious drain on the available labor force. One Vietminh division, in a simple operation, is estimated to have required about 40,000 porters to supply its minimum needs. When one remembers that these divisions had very little heavy equipment and were not motorized (thus requiring no POL°), this was an enormous support force. One of the obvious reasons for the staggering number of porters was the fact that, in addition to army supplies, the porters had to carry their personal provisions. And especially where the lines of communication were long, the coolies' own supplies often made up the bulk of their

° Petroleum, Oil, and Lubricants.

burden. However, there were advantages to this primitive system. Coolies were not only plentiful, but able to travel cross-country, and their easily concealed columns were almost immune to air attack.

*   *   *

In summary, for the better part of the war, when guerrillas and small regular army units were the only elements, logistic needs were limited, and the logistic structure remained quite simple. With the growth of the regular army and the advent of Chinese aid, however, the system became more complex. Developments since the armistice are evidence that the Vietminh recognize logistics as a continuing major problem and are concentrating considerable effort on improving this aspect of their military organization.

IV

OPERATIONS AND TACTICS

A broad political objective underlay the Vietminh's tactics, as it did their strategy. Where Western war aims were merely to occupy a certain territory or to break the will of the enemy, the Viet revolutionaries wanted, above all, to win the support of the populace. In their tactical teachings, they continually emphasized that the goal of an attack was not alone to destroy a given French post but to liberate the inhabitants in the surrounding area and gain their support. "Some of our cadres harbor the mistaken idea," said Giap in 1952, "that armed deeds constitute the only mission of armed forces. They do not focus attention on serving the plan of total conflict and especially propaganda." He went on to complain that this misconception in Vietminh quarters had allowed the enemy to make progress in his propaganda in some areas where the population remained sympathetic to the French, and Viet recruiting, intelligence, and other activities had been correspondingly hampered.

On the strictly military plane, a study of the Vietminh's successes suggests that they rested chiefly on three inter-related factors: (1) a set of five simple tactical principles; (2) full, accurate, and up-to-date intelligence; and (3) detailed planning.

PRINCIPLES AND PREREQUISITES

The Vietminh taught five principles of tactics. The first of these was speed of movement in all phases of combat. Forces were to concentrate quickly, take positions at once, and not linger in any one area. They usually would start from a given point and march for two or three nights to the area of attack, creating a strong element of surprise for the French, who were not aware of the direction of the Viet movements. The position would be developed in one night, and the attack launched in the very early morning. In pursuit, speed was perhaps even more important. "Once the enemy is disorganized," wrote Giap, "it is necessary to ignore fatigue in order automatically to begin the pursuit without awaiting orders." He cited the lack of vigor in the fall campaign of 1950 as a case in which Viet troops had not been sufficiently imbued with motivation for the enemy's total destruction and had thus wasted the sacrifices already made. Giap went further than American doctrine in being willing, if necessary, to forgo reorganization after battle, for he considered it more important to seek to overtake the enemy at once and to continue striking him. If Giap's approach was successful, this was attributable partly to his troops' intense desire to annihilate the enemy (rather than conquer a given piece of terrain). But in part it was due to the fact that the Viet army, being essentially an infantry body, was relatively simple in structure, and reorganization therefore was not a great problem. In retreat, too, speed was all-important. First of all, the Vietminh emphasized, one must never be caught without a way of retreat. The way might be either a definite line from the battle area or a plan by which soldiers would melt into the population and "disappear," sometimes individually and sometimes in small groups. Troops thus dispersed were either reconcentrated later or were left to sustain and aid the guerrillas of the area, depending on the situation.

Surprise, the second principle of Viet tactics, combined the elements of speed, secrecy, and the choice of unsuspected objectives. A favorite device, "intoxication of the enemy," involved a series of deliberate deceptions. The Viet side would deliberately leak information to the enemy that would mislead him into expecting an attack in a certain place at a certain time. To this end, they would make up fake documents and plant them on double agents and on persons who apparently had "rallied" to the French cause. The numerical designation of regular units would be attached to regional units in order to confuse the French. All units would be moved back and forth to give an impression of the movement of large numbers. As mentioned before, night marches that avoided villages and inhabited areas were another means of creating surprise. In a large-scale campaign, all these devices might be employed in combination.

Another tactical principle was to undermine enemy morale in every way possible. Viet agents were infiltrated into French camps to encourage treason and spread propaganda. Also, the Vietminh did not hesitate to make threats against pro-French families. Although Giap was rather reluctant to pay bribes or to use women for blackmail and bribery, these means were not always neglected.

As a general rule, the Vietminh would attack only if the manpower ratio was in their favor, but they believed that with the right combination of surprise and ruse, a highly disciplined small outfit could often prevail over a larger force. They would rely on those means in exceptional circumstances, but only when they felt certain of being able thereby to offset a shortage in manpower.

Much thought was given to security for the Viet forces. Special intelligence units, whose functions were much broader than, for example, those of American intelligence units, played the role of security and reconnaissance forces, and were used to screen regular forces as well as to cover them. They also infiltrated the enemy front to gain information on the preparedness and morale of the enemy. Regional and popular troops were used to protect the regular forces and permit them to fight under the most advantageous conditions. Regional and popular forces, in turn, were covered by small groups with little formal organization, in fact, by the local inhabitants.

The last principle of tactics called for the collaboration of the populace in all military actions. The paradox here is that support from the people was no longer merely an aim of Viet tactics but an integral part of them. A monthly report of the 80th Regiment re-emphasized the importance of this principle by stating that the aim of regimental attacks was not so much to take French posts as to gain control over the population. The 80th Regiment, although part of the regular forces, was detached to a territorial command, and its report specified further that the *raison d'être* of the guerrilla unit, no matter what its size, was to establish and maintain a political-military organization in its area, which formed a basis for regular operations. Giap elaborated on this point in a September, 1952, directive:

> In order to intensify guerrilla activity our attention must be focused not only on the regional troops but also on the armed bases of the communes and the communal guerrillas. The principal question is that of popular troops and the guerrillas. In certain regions one strives to reinforce these troops but is faced with great difficulties. The morale of the population [there] is not as solid as elsewhere. The bases of the popular troops and the cells of the party have been largely annihilated by the enemy and no longer present a satisfactory situation. These armed bases cannot perform their activities and are safeguarded only with great difficulty. Thus, our mission of first priority is to reinforce the popular bases.

On another occasion Giap remarked:

> Guerrilla [warfare] is an armed struggle of all classes of the people. As long as the people do not have a strong hate of the enemy in their hearts, do not have an energetic fighting spirit, as long as the mechanism of the regional authority and the action of the party are not based on a solid organization, one is not able to create a movement for a large battle or for intensified guerrilla action.

In the Vietminh instructions for *Dich Van* groups that have infiltrated enemy-held areas, there is the sentence:

"It is the duty of those who are in the enemy zone to create action around them, to strike the enemy with precision and speed wherever he is, destroying all opponents and appropriating stocks and matériel, and resorting to ambush, attacks, and other measures that create disorder and discontent."

The office of the political commissar for every unit had its propaganda section in charge of psychological warfare. It prepared pamphlets and newspapers for distribution to the civilian population as well as the troops and worked out topics for the propaganda effort of the individual soldier.

A propaganda instruction to the troops that were to invade Laos in 1953 reflects the main themes of Vietminh propaganda directed toward inhabitants of the mountain areas. Beginning with the usual condemnation of French imperialists and their desire to keep all the races of Indochina in slavery, the document goes on to stress the brotherhood of these races and their common cause against colonialism. Ho is portrayed as a kindly and forgiving leader, untiringly working for national independence and the good of all peoples. The propaganda instruction furthermore suggests stressing the army's love for the people and the people's affection for the army, and supplies a long list of ways in which the people might help the army. Reassurance to the natives takes the form of helpful hints on air shelters and other self-defense measures, as well as the promise that on the rare occasions when the army is short of food, the government will pay well for any supplies seized by the troops.

INTELLIGENCE AND RECONNAISSANCE

Not only a careful propaganda plan but painstaking and detailed intelligence coverage formed part of the preparation of every Vietminh operation. Prior to 1948, there were only a *Sûreté* and a Political Intelligence Service, but their findings were not always readily available to the High Command. In response to the growing need for a purely military, operational intelligence service, the *Quan Bao* (Military Intelligence) was formed about 1948.

An elite corps within the army, the *Quan Bao* was composed of Party members who had been especially chosen for their physical, mental, and moral qualifications. After their selection, the recruits went through three months of special training in schools that frequently changed location. Each school had a total of about 150 students. The courses were broadly conceived, and students were subjected to physical conditioning and self-defense, sensory training, background information on the French, and reconnaissance work. As the intelligence corps was also the reconnaissance element of the Vietminh army, the schools placed special stress on the refinement of the physical senses, and future agents were taught to improve their hearing in order to determine not only the direction of a noise but their own distance from it, and learn to distinguish the dominant from lesser noises. Students also learned to observe very quickly and to gauge weight without measuring aids. The course included a whole system of helpful tricks, some of them as elementary as putting an ear to the ground to detect noises, or breathing out before speaking in order to make the voice lower and more distinct. Agents were also instructed in ways to disguise their feelings and were shown how to improve their memory. They learned to write accurate and complete reports, which would give the source as well as the time and circumstances of the matter reported and would include an evaluation by the agent.

After this training, intelligence recruits were assigned to their units. Usually, these were divided into the *Quan Bao*, concerned with intelligence in a narrow sense, and the *Trinh Sat*, responsible for reconnaissance. Companies and battalions had only small *Trinh Sat* units; at regiment and division level, however, there would be intelligence companies, each of which included one *Quan Bao* section and two *Trinh Sat* sections. The *Quan Bao* was the directing element, which planned and co-ordinated the intelligence effort, utilized the information gathered, and for the most part supplied the intelligence officers for the territorial commands and the General Staff.

While the intelligence service employed such comparatively modern methods as radio intercept and triangulation as means of obtaining information, it counted heavily on direct personal interrogation of both the local civilians and enemy personnel, and its training schools therefore emphasized the value of obtaining prisoners. Special groups, organized to launch attacks for the express purpose of capturing prisoners, usually comprised four subsections: a fire group, which was to cause confusion in the enemy ranks; a capturing group, which rounded up the prisoners; a support group, which helped the capturing group and watched for reinforcements; and an escort group, which took the prisoners to the rear for interrogation. In addition to these more or less formal assaults, the Vietminh resorted also to ambush and surprise attacks on small units and tried to seize isolated soldiers wherever possible.

From all accounts, the Vietminh were psychologically very adept at interrogation. They would interview prisoners of war two or three times, for long periods at a stretch, and preferably at hours when the prisoners' resistance was lowest. They had been taught to be very objective, and to approach the prisoners without any show of preconceived ideas. A favorite practice was to employ irony or sarcasm, which tended to make the prisoner lose his patience and give out more information than he intended. Sometimes, Viet agents would be slipped into prisoners' cells or enclosures. According to accounts by French prisoners, the Vietminh seldom resorted to force.

As the war went on, intelligence units took over more and more, though not all, of the reconnaissance and security duties formerly performed by the regional and popular troops. At battalion, regiment, and division level, intelligence units provided cover for the movements of these forces as well as the reconnaissance for all operations. In the effort to obtain information they used all possible devices: they would disguise themselves to infiltrate enemy areas, send armed patrols to contact the enemy and ascertain the location of his positions, and engage in combat if it promised to yield valuable information.

Anyone familiar with United States army reconnaissance would recognize many of the Vietminh reconnaissance functions, but there were also some rather important differences. Responsible for the security of the troops, reconnaissance units reconnoitered both retreat and advance routes and searched for places suitable for ambush. Agents were planted in suspect zones to keep the units informed. Both the teaching and the execution of camouflage were among the functions of Viet reconnaissance. After combat, it was up to the reconnaissance units to discover what losses the Vietminh had suffered and what arms had been taken from the enemy. Also, at this point, they were responsible for recording their own mistakes, leading troops back to the concentration area, guarding the prisoners, and authorizing civilians to return to their homes armed with propaganda. For units in camp, they had to investigate the cooking areas, examine gifts from the local people, and keep a check on relations between troops and native population. It was their duty, furthermore, to guard automatic weapons as well as documents, to keep an eye on soldiers in public places, and to prevent desertion. On festive occasions, they were responsible for the behavior and discipline of the troops in town, at the same time that they had to post guards and lookouts for enemy aircraft and prepare for quick evacuation in case of attack.

Captured Vietminh documents have brought to light painstaking intelligence surveys of French troop dispositions, habits, and activities, which obviously served the Vietminh as a very good planning base for their operations. One intelligence study prepared by the Vietminh for their northwestern operations in 1952 impressed the French greatly by its scope as well as by the detail and accuracy of the information. The document included a very careful survey of the terrain and its trafficability for all types of vehicles and for coolies. It also contained an objective study of the various tribes in the area and their attitudes toward the Vietminh and the French. Part of this section was given over to a detailed description of the Vietminh's secret bases in the area and to a loyalty estimate of the people in them. In the Gia Hoi–Sai Luong base, for instance, ninety persons were marked down as Vietminh sympathizers, of whom thirty were regarded as completely reliable. Again, in the Phu Nhan–Son Thin area, there were twenty-five faithful adherents scattered through several villages. The study concluded by stating that, although these figures did not add up to strong popular support, the bases did offer a certain hospitality to the Vietminh troops.

The Infantry and the Mobility Factor

Vietminh tactics were essentially infantry tactics. A significant amount of artillery became available only in the last months of the war, and armor was lacking throughout. But even had there been the heavy equipment that the Vietminh continued to wish for, armor and artillery obviously had very limited mobility in an underdeveloped country with the difficult terrain of Indochina. Furthermore, Giap realized that it was quicker and easier to turn a guerrilla into an infantryman than into a tanker or artilleryman.

The Viet army's heavy reliance on infantry meant, first

of all, that their combat units were not encumbered with many tanks or much artillery and that the battle corps was more or less free of combat trains and heavy service units. The army was thus quite mobile and not tied to particular areas or bases. By the same token, it was not bound to stick to the roads, but could execute cross-country marches with considerable ease and speed and managed to perform great feats of infiltration. Finally, this primarily infantry army was able to escape detection and attack from the air.

Mobility—in offensive as well as defensive action—was the key to all operations, from the small actions of the guerrillas to the larger campaigns of the regular forces. As mentioned earlier, the regular forces were rarely permitted to accept battle in unfavorable situations, and were supposed to slip away when in danger of attack from superior French forces. These tactics were essentially like those of guerrillas, who strike and run and avoid battles at almost any cost. But unlike the guerrillas, who hit in order to cause confusion, destroy certain property, and keep the enemy off balance, the regular forces struck to annihilate.

THE OFFENSIVE

The Viets taught that there were four important prerequisites for a successful attack: the proper choice of time, a careful plan, adequate preparation, and high combative spirit.

Timing of the attack was obviously dependent on the time needed for planning and for concentrating the troops, as well as on the general situation. To a great extent, however, it also depended on the enemy. When the Viets decided to attack a post or fort, it was not just a matter of preparing a plan and then executing it. They would watch the garrison over a period of time in order to discover enemy habits and weaknesses. For instance, they would try to determine when the guards were changed, whether certain guards were habitually not alert, and at what times key officers or noncoms might be expected to be absent; and they would look for any signs of complacency or laxity among members of the garrison. All such intelligence information was then incorporated in the final plan, which specified time and locale of the main effort, points of secondary attacks, installations to be neutralized by firepower, and provisions for retreat. Each subordinate unit was assigned a specific job, and all details were worked out and discussed with the officers and noncoms. Sometimes the Vietminh would have a rehearsal of the attack, using specially constructed facsimiles of the French post or fort. All necessary equipment, arms, and ammunition having been procured, the Viets then set about explaining to the troops the reason for the attack and the importance of its success, rousing them to a high pitch of fanaticism and self-sacrifice, for a combat spirit equal to the task at hand was regarded as an indispensable element in the preparations.

The Viet units often moved to and from the battlefields by infiltration, which they practiced with great skill, thereby escaping air and ground detection and avoiding the danger of providing a target for air attack. They often infiltrated right through the French units so as to create greater surprise by attacking the enemy from both sides. The French have estimated that the Viets could infiltrate several individuals through a zone with a 1,300-yard perimeter, several platoons if the perimeter was 2,200 yards, and several companies where it was 4,400 yards long. If the perimeter was still longer, they might succeed in infiltrating a battalion and even a regiment. The Hanoi Delta perimeter, for example, with its posts about two-thirds of a mile apart, had virtually no protection against Vietminh infiltration.*

The Vietminh usually attacked at night, because this gave them several advantages over the French. Not only were the French considered poor night fighters, but they lacked air support, and the darkness made artillery support difficult. A typical attack would begin at midnight or soon thereafter and break off at nine or ten in the morning. Whenever possible, the Viets would aim at complete surprise, often giving up preparatory fires to that end. The main effort, sometimes as much as nine-tenths of the attacking force, usually was concentrated on a very narrow front. The remainder made diversionary and noisy attacks, often before the main assault (especially if surprise was impossible to achieve), and their firepower would be directed at a few critical points.

Normally, four groups were involved in the attack. The first of these manned the heavy supporting weapons (usually automatic weapons, mortars, and recoilless rifles), whose aim was to neutralize one or two important enemy

---

* However, French artillery, with massed preplanned fires, was able to stop attacks and large-scale attempts at penetration.

positions, such as the radio, the command post, or heavy weapons. If the attack were unsuccessful, their fire was to cover the retreat. The second group would be the assault engineers or dynamiters. These men, who might be a company or a platoon, ran forward or infiltrated the enemy lines and exploded dynamite in critical areas of the fort or post so as to create a breach. Leaving all personal weapons behind in their trenches, the dynamiters were armed only with explosives, which they sometimes carried on the ends of bamboo poles that could be forced into wire entanglements, and on occasion even tied to their own bodies in order to hurl themselves with the charges into enemy wire or walls. If they were able to return, they retrieved their weapons and assisted in the general attack. Once the enemy weapons had been neutralized and the dynamiters had created a breach, the third group—shock troops or assault infantry—moved forward, usually in three groups and on a narrow front, and attempted to overwhelm the post. The fourth was a reserve group, which covered the shock troops with fire, assisted in the attack, and either exploited the success or covered the retreat.

Although fighting from within the enemy positions was admittedly difficult, the Vietminh felt that it could be done successfully if four principles were observed: (1) Careful planning and training were essential. The planning was usually done with the aid of sand boards or other replicas of the French posts, and the attack was rehearsed many times. (2) In order to destroy the main enemy installations, the troops had to penetrate as deeply as possible and could not allow themselves to be kept out on the

periphery of the fort. (3) There had to be close co-operation and co-ordination among the dynamiters, fire-support
units, and shock troops. (4) A successful operation required close liaison between the attacking unit and its
regiment and neighboring units.

The Vietminh were careful, also, to anticipate strong
enemy reactions and counterattacks. Counterattacks, especially, were considered excellent opportunities to destroy
an enemy who had left his shelter, and special plans were
made for this contingency. On the other hand, Viet tactical
doctrine demanded that if the Viets' own attacking troops
were caught in three enemy fires, they concentrate on one
and ignore the other two. Whenever they were themselves
caught by a frontal attack, they were to avoid the strong
places and counterattack the weak. When stopped by an
artillery barrage, they were instructed either to retreat,
dig in, and await artillery support, or if they were close to
the enemy, to "cling" to him. When cut off or encircled,
they were to try either to break through at one point or to
disband and seek their way out individually.

The Vietminh believed (and their training instructions
said so quite explicitly) that if the secret of an impending
attack was well kept and the action instantaneous, even a
handful of lightly equipped but well-armed assailants,
under cover of night or expert camouflage, could sometimes smash a numerically superior enemy even in an
attack on a post. This presupposed being informed to the
hour and even to the minute of all activities in the post,
so as to be able to profit from the moment when the
enemy relaxed his watch in order to launch the attack.

Controlling the Lines of Communication

Much of the war effort on both sides was devoted to the battle for communications. The Vietminh tried to paralyze the French by denying them the use of roads, paths, and waterways. The greatest part of guerrilla activity was devoted to mining and destroying roads. In certain areas, the Vietminh regularly cut the roads at night and the French attempted to repair them during the day. Nearly everywhere, French soldiers had to check the roads for mines and cuts every morning before they could be used.

The ambush was the Vietminh's favorite means of attack on communications. This was not a spur-of-the-moment tactic but entailed considerable planning and preparation. Not only did guerrillas and regional troops ambush isolated French vehicles and units, but there were major ambushes of larger French formations. The Vietminh particularly liked to ambush relief units, using the following tactics: A stationary element, often composed of one company (which we shall call the "second element"), would straddle the road at a given point, where it could effectively block off any advance. Approximately 500 to 1,000 yards farther in the direction from which the relief column was coming, the "first element," composed of perhaps five units, was placed on both sides of the road. Finally, a "third element," about three companies strong and called the "rear ambush," waited at a distance of still another 1,000 yards behind the first element. Positions were care-

fully chosen and weapons artfully concealed. As the reliev-
ing force advanced down the road, it passed unhindered
and unsuspecting by the third and first elements, but was
stopped by the second element blocking the road. As soon
as it was demobilized, the other two elements struck. The
major element, in the middle, attacked the main force,
while the third element, in the rear, attempted to cut off
any retreat as well as possible relief forces.* The French
have complained that, in spite of air and other observation means, they found it almost impossible to detect these
ambushes and were nearly always trapped in them. The
only defense against them was to devise means of reducing
their effectiveness. Sometimes the French would make
their columns longer than the stretch covered by the ambushing elements, thereby enabling part of their forces to
escape and another part to come to the rescue of the
trapped units. Also, they equipped the relief columns with
artillery and armor to help rout the rebels. Then, too, they
discovered that they could send a single vehicle, and even
two or three vehicles, down the road without having them
molested by the Vietminh, who were waiting for larger
prey. During clearing operations, they tried to provide air
cover, which, they hoped, would discover or discourage
any ambush. Most of these measures, however, fell short
of success, and the French lived in fear of ambushes to
the end of the war.

* Obviously not every Viet ambush followed this pattern to the letter.
This illustration is provided chiefly to show the care and planning that
went into a typical ambush.

THE DEFENSIVE

Following the precepts of Mao, "If the enemy attacks, I disappear; if he defends, I harass; and if he retreats, I attack," the Vietminh avoided defensive combat whenever possible. The fact that their few vital installations were in distant and difficult areas beyond the reach of French ground forces usually allowed them to refuse combat if they wished.

Vietminh units, no matter what positions they were in, had plans for retreat. A classic example of this tactic was furnished in August, 1948, on the Plaine des Joncs, a great swampy area in Cochinchina. The French had discovered the location of the command post of Nguyen Binh, the Viet commander of Cochinchina, and mounted a land and air operation with the objective of seizing or killing him and his staff. Several battalions plowed through the mud, while more than two companies of paratroopers jumped right on the command post. Surprise was complete. A few shots were fired at the paratroopers as they descended and a short skirmish ensued as they landed, but almost immediately, at a given signal, all combat broke off. The Viet enemy just disappeared, and neither the surrounding French land forces nor the paratroopers could find any of the defenders. It was clear that the Vietminh had detailed plans for such an occasion and had executed them perfectly.

There were two possible methods for disappearing. One was to retreat into previously prepared hiding places in the area, such as subterranean caves, specially constructed holes, and positions prepared in the banks of rivers and originating below the water level. All such places were cleverly camouflaged, and only very few persons knew of their location. The other method was to retreat in small groups or individually, and either disappear into the woods or melt into the population of a neighboring village or city.

When the Vietminh did decide to defend a place, they proceeded by a very careful plan. Their techniques and tactics of defense were best illustrated in the villages. Having decided to defend a given village, they would work out a detailed program for its fortification and active defense. Individual shelter and hiding places, usually underground and connected by tunnels, were constructed in such a way that a defender could fire from one place, disappear, and then fire from another. Some of the individual holes were supplied with food and water, in case concealment was necessary for several days. They were so well camouflaged that the French often used dogs to sniff them out, and the Viets, in turn, had to use lime in the entrances to stop the dogs. Even good fields of fire often were sacrificed for the sake of better camouflage, and the defenders were allowed to disclose the location of their hiding places only to their leaders.

Villages in the Tonkin were already partially fortified against pirates and animals, and the Vietminh improved these existing defenses by adding antitank obstacles, mines, and other modern devices. During the first years of the war, they tried to make every village impregnable, but they soon realized that this was impossible, and restricted themselves to making it as difficult as possible

for the enemy to advance into a village. Their first fortified villages all had identical defense plans, as the French
soon found out. Thereafter, the Viet varied their plans for
defense and thus complicated the attackers' problem.

A network of guards protected each such village and
the sectors within it. During daylight hours the guards,
disguised as peasants or workers, were placed at a half-
mile to a mile from the village. Their positions were
changed frequently, and a messenger, also in disguise, was
always at hand to take news of an enemy advance to the
village. At night the guards were pulled in closer to the
village and posted near the gates. Each sector had its own
guard system and an accepted warning signal. At all times
strangers were watched and their credentials carefully
checked. There were liaison channels to neighboring
villages and higher headquarters.

The Viets made every effort to confuse the French as to
the location of the defenders, and often enticed them into
prepared traps, where they were then surrounded. When
attacked, the village defenders were to hit at the enemy
continuously as he approached, entered, and penetrated
the village. It was not expected that the enemy would be
annihilated in the initial phase. As soon as he weakened,
however, a counterattack was launched with the aim of
annihilation. If, on the other hand, the French continued
to press forward, retreat would be ordered.

In the defense of villages, as in all situations, the Vietminh, reluctant to lose even irregular guerrillas, laid careful plans for retreat. In a hopeless fight, the defenders were
instructed, upon a prearranged signal for disengagement,

to retreat to their holes or abandon the villages by routes indicated in advance.

The Case of Dien Bien Phu

The battle of Dien Bien Phu deserves special mention, as it was not typical of the fighting in Indochina. In the autumn of 1953, the French government determined that Laos should be defended and, almost simultaneously, negotiated a defense treaty with the Laotian government. The French commander in Indochina, General Henri Navarre, was instructed to defend Laos but not to endanger the safety of the Expeditionary Corps. Navarre knew he could not defend Laos by a war of movement or by any defensive line and decided that the only way was to establish a strategically located aero-ground strong point, which, he hoped, would prevent a massive invasion. Furthermore, there was some expectation that Giap's forces would thereby be drawn into a set battle with resulting heavy casualties for the Vietminh. He recognized, however, that such a strong point would not prevent all enemy military movements into Laos.

The village of Dien Bien Phu—located in a valley roughly ten by five miles and more than two hundred miles from the French air bases in Hanoi and Vientiane—was selected as the site for this strong point and was occupied late in November, 1953. Although Navarre recognized that this was not the ideal site for such an operation, he considered it the best in the area. He was criticized at the time for selecting Dien Bien Phu, and has been since, for this meant that the enemy would occupy all the surrounding high ground. French air force officers have also stated that had they been consulted, the position would not have been agreed to, as it was at the extreme range of the fighter aircraft which were to support the base. The controversy over these points continued even after the war and can never really be resolved, though—with the wisdom of hindsight—Navarre's critics may be said to have been correct in their assessment of the position.

The French seriously underestimated the artillery available to the Vietminh and the method in which it would be employed. The Chinese had provided Giap with far more regular artillery than French intelligence knew. But the most significant development was that the Vietminh used their artillery in direct fire, and not indirectly, as the French—and for that matter American—artillerymen had predicted. Instead of positioning behind the hills, which would have put the French forts out of range, the Vietminh moved their guns at night onto the forward slopes of the hills. There they carefully dug in and camouflaged single pieces, which were fired point-blank at the French, and with devastating effect. Using this tactic, the Vietminh soon knocked out or neutralized the French artillery and thus were able to creep closer to the French forts and launch massive attacks. With the French artillery out of commission, the Vietminh were then able to bring their own antiaircraft guns much closer to the forts and thus make air resupply very difficult and dangerous. Indeed, by April, only parachute drops were possible, and those at successively higher altitudes. The French fighter aircraft, which could remain in the area for only a short time because of range limitations, had to be used mainly for flank suppression instead of close support.

A second major miscalculation of the French was that Giap would not engage in a siege operation. But this is exactly what he did in fact undertake. A special road was constructed to the Dien Bien Phu area, so that supplies could be brought directly from China; and, beginning in December and January, supplies and ammunition were stocked for a long siege. The French-led mountain tribes that were to sabotage the Vietminh supply routes failed completely in this mission. As the Vietminh artillery smashed the French artillery and defenses, Giap pushed forward a complex system of trenches and dugouts. French aerial photography of the area in February and March revealed a mass of trenches that tightened increasingly around the beleaguered forts in the manner of a true eighteenth-century siege.

In March, after artillery supremacy had been largely gained and supplies assembled, Giap launched the first of his massive attacks on Dien Bien Phu. Gabrielle and Béatrice, the two outposts on the high ground within the valley, were the first to fall under the waves of Giap's massed infantry. The loss of these forts confirmed to the defenders that Giap had in fact gained full artillery supremacy and that they could not effectively reply to his fire.

In May, the Vietminh launched the attack that finally overran the position, and on May 8, the last French troops surrendered. Thus the battle of Dien Bien Phu was over and Giap had won a decisive victory.

French casualties, including prisoners, totaled about 12,000 men, which was only about 6 per cent of the total expeditionary force. Giap's casualties were numerically probably twice those of the French. Though the loss of Dien Bien Phu and its garrison was a bitter and unexpected defeat for France and a blow to Western strength, it was not in the military sense a decisive one. Its main impact was in the political arena, where it was sufficient to persuade the French to negotiate and end the war.

V

VIETMINH REACTIONS TO FRENCH TACTICS AND AIR POWER

Particularly important in a study of this nature are the responses of each side to new tactics and techniques of the other. The present chapter will deal primarily with Vietminh reactions to French innovations, but it will examine also some of the ways in which the French responded to the tactics and countertactics of the Vietminh.

Undermining the Policy of Pacification

Until 1950, the major effort of the French was in the south, in Cochinchina, the region of their greatest successes. Here the French had adopted a policy of pacification, with the threefold aim of crushing rebel bands, helping the local people establish defenses of their own, and restoring normal life to the villages and cities. Pacification thus had both a military and a political aspect. While there was considerable military success, the French tended to fall short on the political side. Their reluctance to grant independence to Vietnam and their frequent failure to follow up military successes by re-establishing regular administration and services in the pacified regions prevented their victories from being clear-cut and permanent.

From a military point of view, pacification actions were mainly of two types: sweeping operations, to clear an area between two or more points held by the French; and extending operations, to spread French control further out into Vietminh territory. The pacification forces, which varied in size from a few companies to several battalions, were made up primarily of infantry, but included also engineers, artillerymen, and tanks. They usually operated in columns, as the nature of their equipment and armament forced them to stick to such primary means of communication as roads or dikes. This requirement not only exposed them to certain Vietminh tactics but limited the effectiveness of their actions. Occasionally, the French engaged in sweeping operations in which the infantry would comb the countryside. However, in swampy terrain and mountainous or forested regions, this was exceedingly slow and difficult, and the enemy usually escaped. Quite often, the French tried first to cut off all means of escape by encirclement and then to sweep the enclosed area, but the Viets' skill at infiltration frequently foiled these efforts.

Certain other factors contributed to making these operations less successful than they might have been. French intelligence was poor and most Vietminh areas seemed to have forewarning of the enemy's coming. The French soldiers frequently conducted themselves in a manner that alienated the native population, and did not seem to realize the importance of winning the local people to their side through positive acts. As already pointed out, inadequate political follow-up of military victory slowed down the return to normal administrative life in villages and towns in which French control had been re-established. The French also were a long time developing an adequate psychological program for either the civilians or the military. Finally, the difficult terrain and debilitating weather proved a serious hindrance to the French advance.

Nevertheless, pacification made considerable headway in the south, particularly before 1950. Recognizing it as a threat, the Vietminh devised tactics to undermine it. First and most important was the political counteraction. Viet agents would infiltrate a village or an area and establish a cell, which became the center for counterpacification, spreading propaganda and recruiting adherents to the Vietminh cause among the population. Having once gained a foothold and won some support for the struggle against the French, the Vietminh would proceed more aggressively. They often attacked and killed natives who attempted to co-operate with the French or to oppose Vietminh penetration. These examples succeeded in terrifying the local people and proved a strong deterrent to pro-French activity in the area.

PUTTING THE FRENCH ON THE DEFENSIVE

On the military side, the Vietminh improved defenses or fortified the villages so as to make French clearing operations more difficult. Also, since they especially feared the French encircling actions, they issued detailed instructions on counterencirclement tactics. On the major points,

these followed the general tactical rules that Viet combatants must try to avoid any conflict not in their favor or,
if caught in a tight encirclement, must concentrate on the
weak point of the encircling forces and fight their way
through. The manuals stressed again and again that encircling forces were never strong at all points and that a
determined attack could always effect a break. If in danger
of being encircled by a particularly strong French force
on easy terrain, the Viet units were urged to withdraw
from the area in time and leave no one for the French
to capture.

Developments in the Tonkin area in the north were a
particularly good example of Viet military countertactics
that succeeded in forcing the enemy from the offensive
into a defensive posture. While the French had occupied
certain border positions in order to cut the Vietminh off
from Chinese aid, their primary aim was to create a stronghold in the Red River Delta region that would not only
serve as a secure operational base but would also enable
them to cut off the Viet food supply and thus force the
Vietminh to fight for it in the Delta. To this end, General
de Lattre attempted to form a front, in the Western sense,
composed of forts and posts, the smallest of which were
only about half a mile apart, while the larger "mother"
forts were spaced at several miles from one another. The
forts ranged from simple towers, surrounded by barbed
wire and held by a few dozen men, to elaborate fortifications with heavy arms and garrisoned by several hundred
men. However, the French recognized that static defenses
alone were rarely successful, and, furthermore, De Lattre
had no intention of assuming a defensive posture. Once

the base had been made secure, fortifications properly provided, and the forces redeployed, so-called "mobile groups," composed of infantry, armor, and artillery and representing the cream of the French troops, were to be used as offensive striking forces to attack key Vietminh installations and force combat on their own terms. This strategy, however, was foiled by a series of Viet tactics, which succeeded in tying up so many French troops that only few offensive actions could be undertaken, and the French posture remained essentially defensive.

After their surprising victory on the border posts in 1950, the Vietminh at first had continued to launch major attacks around the edges of the Red River Delta but had given up when they suffered heavy casualties. Thereafter, they infiltrated large units, up to division size, through the French posts and forts to assist their guerrillas within the Delta. It was said that the French held the Delta in the daytime and the Vietminh held it at night. Even within this center of the French defenses, the Viets used mines and ambushes, and destroyed portions of roads, in order to disrupt French civilian and military traffic. There was excellent co-ordination between the clandestine activities inside and the operations of the Vietminh forces outside the Delta, and guerrilla activity within was intensified whenever the French struck at the Vietminh outside. It has been reliably estimated that in 1953 about 35,000 Vietminh were tying up three times their number of French forces in the Delta. As in the counterpacification effort in the south, the Viets made examples of individuals in order to frighten any natives who might want to support the French. They also attacked many of the posts or forts, particularly the more isolated ones. These were usually surprise night attacks, which had been carefully planned, with high superiority in manpower. After the arrival of Chinese aid, and with it some heavier guns, the Viets were able to use armor-piercing shells against the forts, many of which were old and somewhat flimsily constructed and could not stand up against this type of action.

The French, of course, did not accept these counter-tactics passively. They brought in dogs from France, which they used to detect the approach of any enemy, particularly during the night, but the dogs were often unable to distinguish between friend and foe. On a very limited scale, the French attempted to reduce the difficulties of night combat by illuminating the area after dark, but their supply of equipment was inadequate for this purpose. Then, also, they constructed their newer forts underground, with just a few observation points above ground. This did indeed make attacks more difficult and the use of armor-piercing shells less effective, but most forts, unless relieved by mobile columns, fell before a determined Vietminh attack.

In the course of the war, as the Vietminh developed their offensive power, including units large enough to undertake major operations, the French were put more and more on the defensive, and were forced to find ways of countering certain Vietminh tactics and techniques by developing new techniques of their own. One of their most important innovations was to create what they called "air-ground strong points" in the mountain areas controlled by the Vietminh but inhabited by people generally sympathetic to the French. Since the French needed to keep some troops and strong points in these areas, and their land communications were extremely unreliable, they put individual garrisons in the vicinity of their airstrips and supplied them by air. With these strong points as bases, and sometimes with paratroop support, they were able to beat off many Vietminh attacks and maintain the French "presence." However, the small number of available cargo planes and the great need for French troops in the Delta limited the number of troops that could be used in strong points, as was shown, of course, at Dien Bien Phu.

A second countertechnique, based on the experience gained in France during World War II, was to form partisan groups in the mountainous areas to act as a maquis against the Vietminh. During the battle of Dien Bien Phu, the French claim to have had in the area the equivalent of about fifteen battalions of partisan guerrillas who were to have interfered with Vietminh supply lines. The action remained very limited, and most French officers were disappointed at the results. But it is true that on several occasions the Vietminh had to detach regiments to clean out areas where the French had penetrated with their guerrillas.

NEUTRALIZATION OF AIR POWER

Throughout the war, the Vietminh admitted that one of the greatest advantages of the French was that of air power and, indeed, of absolute air superiority. Having acknowledged this, however, they explained in numerous manuals and propaganda pamphlets how this French advantage could be neutralized. Before examining how they went about minimizing the effects of French air power, it is well to look briefly at the kind of air power the French had in Indochina, the manner in which they employed it, and the difficulties of operation under which they labored. While published statistics are inexact, the following seems to be a fairly accurate estimate of French aircraft in Indochina: In November, 1951, there were 158 fighters, 42 light bombers, 75 transports, 28 reconnaissance planes, and 105 light aircraft. Two years later, in November, 1953, the French had 120 fighters, 42 light bombers, 84 transports, 16 reconnaissance craft, and approximately 237 other planes, including light craft and trainers. In March, 1954, at the beginning of the battle of Dien Bien Phu, there were 123 fighters plus 40 carrier-borne fighters, 41 light bombers, 124 transports, 16 reconnaissance planes, and 230 other aircraft.* These figures did not include some hired civilian cargo planes, which helped with air supply.

The French air force in Indochina operated under severe difficulties. In the first place, there were only about five first-class airfields, a fact which, from the beginning, put a ceiling on the number of aircraft that could be operated in this theater. It was extremely difficult to construct new airfields. In the delta regions, it was said to take one ton of crushed rock for every square yard of runway, and this rock had to be allowed to settle slowly. As a result, even under a "crash" program, airfields could not safely be constructed quickly. The mountain areas were generally in Vietminh hands and, besides, presented

* General L. M. Chassin, *Aviation Indochine* (*Air Power in Indochina*) (Amiot-Dumont: Paris, 1954).

construction problems of their own. The second major difficulty in planning for French air operations was that the weather was bad much of the year and varied greatly from one part of Indochina to another. There were few weather stations, and even if the weather was good at Hanoi, it might not be good over the target or between target and take-off point. Thirdly, the French air force complained that their maps were unreliable. Heights of peaks and other essential terrain information were inaccurate, and in certain areas, therefore, planes could not operate safely. And last of all, radio guidance and navigational aids were inadequate for normal flying, and still more so for night and bad-weather operations.

French air force officers were almost unanimous in their criticism of the command structure. Serving under an army commander in chief who was responsible for the entire Indochina theater, they felt that they were rarely involved in the planning and that had they been consulted, many operations would have been carried out differently and more effectively. They believed that, in general, air power was misused. One of their complaints was that it was tied too much to the army; it was, for example, often used for direct support when it could more properly have been employed for interdiction and other air targets.

Since the Vietminh did not have any air force, the battle for air superiority never came into play; to the end of the war, the French were able to use their air power in every way they chose, including interdiction, direct support of the army, air supply, and the launching of airborne operations.

Vietminh antiaircraft capability improved in the course

of the war, especially after the advent of Chinese aid. During the siege of Dien Bien Phu, as we have seen, the Viets were able to knock down a number of French planes and to keep most of the others at altitudes too high for effective assistance and accurate supply drops to the troops. Though apparently antiaircraft guns were not radar-controlled, there were some excellent Russian pieces that were skillfully used. Even before they acquired anti-aircraft, however, the Vietminh had managed to shoot down quite a few planes simply with rifles and machine guns, and guerrillas had tried to incapacitate planes on the ground. It is interesting to note that the Vietminh attacked chiefly the transport planes and rarely molested the fighters.

While the French had made sporadic interdiction efforts all along, it was not until 1952 that they really planned an extensive interdiction program against the Vietminh's supply routes, particularly those leading from the Chinese border. In this campaign, they concentrated on two types of targets: truck garages and warehouses where supplies might be stored, and difficult stretches of road that were hard to bypass. Most of their targets were within the Lang Son–Bac Kan–Cao Bang triangle. The French air force made much of the success of this offensive and, at one time, claimed to have reduced the flow of Chinese aid from 1,500 to 250 tons a month. The Vietminh reacted to this intensified interdiction effort in several ways, none of them particularly novel. In the first place, as most trans-portation took place at night and the French had prac-tically no night capability, the coolies remained relatively safe then. If the tactical situation on the battlefield made it necessary to move during daylight hours, coolies tried, whenever possible, to employ unknown paths and new routes. This made the French air effort more difficult, since small paths with coolie columns were very hard to spot, and the French reconnaissance capability had declined by 1952. At critical points on the roads, the Vietminh sometimes stationed repair crews that would rebuild any bridges that were destroyed. At other times, they merely used boats to move the supplies across.

Direct air support for the French ground forces was used to a considerable extent. Many of the French themselves have felt that this was a mistake in view of its admittedly limited value. Except in battle, the Vietminh units were extremely difficult to locate, as they were usually well dug in and were very artful when it came to dispersal, camouflage, and concealment. Also, they would often mingle with the populace, and the French air force either could not distinguish them from the civilians or, if it could, was unable to strike at them for fear of hitting some of the village or city people. Vietminh attacks, as stated earlier, always began at night, when the French air force had very limited capability. If the battle continued into the daylight hours, an effective method by which the Viets avoided air attack was to "cling" to the enemy, that is, to stay so close to the French forces that air fire would hit both friend and foe.

In the final stage of the war, air supply of the French garrisons became increasingly important and lacked only an adequate number of transport aircraft to have been still more effective. The French advantage in air supply went virtually unchallenged in view of the opponent's limited antiaircraft capability. The Vietminh made every effort to infiltrate agents into French air bases, and even the most heavily guarded planes were found sabotaged. During the battle of Dien Bien Phu, when air supply was keeping the French garrison going, the Vietminh, in a noteworthy example of co-ordination in their war effort, conducted a special sabotage campaign in the Delta to destroy these cargo planes. It was indicative of the importance they attached to the air supply capability of the French.

Though airborne operations were important in Indochina, the limited French airlift capability precluded large operations. Usually only one battalion, and even in the latter stages of the war never more than two or three battalions, could be airlifted for a single operation. Despite this, the French rarely achieved surprise, for their reconnaissance planes surveying the area prior to attack, and the advance of French ground units toward a given area, would often alert the Vietminh to a possible airborne attack. Also, the very nature of the war made paratroop operations less effective than they would have been in a conventional war. As there was no front, there was nobody to cut off, and paratroopers therefore were usually employed against a key point with the hope of destroying it. In most cases, a battalion proved too small to do the job, particularly during the latter phases of the war, when the Vietminh units were large. Occasional plans to have the paratroopers link up with the ground forces usually produced disappointing results.

Nevertheless, the Vietminh feared airborne operations and took precautions against them. All of their units, fortified villages, and other important areas posted guards whose mission it was to look out for aircraft, and particularly paratroopers. In certain spots that seemed especially suitable for landings, the Vietminh put up pointed bamboo sticks on which the paratroopers would impale themselves. Then again, if threatened by paratroop attack, the Viets would just disappear and leave no one for the paratroopers to fight. And lastly, the French were compelled to gather up their chutes after every jump, and one-fourth to one-third of the jumping unit would be tied up in this task, often for half a day, reducing the number of effectives who were free to fight. The Vietminh took advantage of this opportunity to attack the chute collectors and thus make the landing more difficult and costly in lives.

❃   ❃   ❃

As in all wars, there was thus a constant interplay between the combatants: Each devised new tactics and strategies and the other attempted to foil them. The Vietminh were seldom slow to spot a new French tactic and to issue instructions on how to counter it. The French were somewhat less flexible and tended to adhere to their accustomed methods of warfare even when these were no longer paying off.

VI

POSTARMISTICE MILITARY DEVELOPMENTS

By Anne M. Jonas*

Under the terms of the 1954 Geneva cease-fire agreements, which ended the war between the French and the Vietminh, Vietnam was partitioned and a Communist state was created in the northern sector. General Giap became Minister of Defense of this newly established Democratic Republic of Vietnam. The military forces under his command now were confronted with a far more diversified set of assignments than those of the war years. The troops were expected to assist in the general effort to repair war damage and to build up the economy. Border areas had to be policed, political indoctrination expanded, and other measures taken to ensure the regime's consolidation and maintenance of its control over the population. Furthermore, the guerrillas were required to continue clandestine infiltration and terror operations in nearby countries. It was equally necessary to utilize the time gained by the existence of a formal cease-fire to improve the fighting capabilities of the regular forces. Now there was an op-

* Other commitments prevented the principal author from completing his research for this chapter. Anne M. Jonas, of the Social Science Department of The RAND Corporation, kindly consented to undertake the work.

portunity to intensify their training, discipline and ideological indoctrination; to standardize and modernize
organization and matériel; to improve logistics lines and to
erect fortifications. There also was a requirement to create
a trained reserve, nonexistent during the war.

None of these missions could be accomplished quickly,
and all had to be undertaken more or less simultaneously.
It is not surprising, therefore, that seven years after the
armistice, the Vietminh military establishment still is in a
state of transition. Gradually, however, a more formal
organizational structure and a more clear-cut division of
labor between its various elements is emerging. The ultimate goal is to maintain, at all times, a battle-ready
regular force, a trained reserve, and a sufficient number of
guerrillas to meet any future contingency. But the drive
for an improved military and paramilitary capability has
not reduced the preoccupation with preparing every
soldier for a dual role. Political work and direct participation in efforts to increase the nation's economic productivity remain as much a part of his duties as ever.

How well have the military forces succeeded in adapting themselves to the environment in which they have
operated since mid-1954? How effective have they been
in carrying out their various assignments? In order to
arrive at an evaluation, it is necessary to examine, in turn,
the current functions of the guerrillas, the efforts being
made to improve the regular forces, the evolution of a
trained reserve, the role of the military in implementing
domestic political and economic policy, and the contributions North Vietnam's military establishment has made to
the revolutionary war in Laos.

The Guerrillas Today

The guerrillas now are organized into militia units, stationed primarily in the border areas, and into special clandestine groups operating within the regular army. Reform measures gradually have improved the capabilities of the regular forces for waging overt war, should the need arise, and for carrying out the military's domestic political and economic responsibilities. Therefore, the guerrillas have been increasingly freed to concentrate on covert functions outside North Vietnam.

However, the transition is not yet completed. The militia, at least, still is expected not only to engage in infiltration operations, but also to carry out certain tasks at home. But many of these domestic functions, essential as they are, merely serve to disguise the guerrillas' principal current mission: clandestine infiltration. Infiltration operations now are monitored by the Party's Central Committee, and more and more importance is being attached to them.

All covert activities since 1954 have exploited the fact that the North Vietnamese guerrillas easily can pose as nationals of surrounding countries. Boundary lines in Southeast Asia are poorly demarcated and were drawn with little regard for tribal and ethnic ties. Accurate census figures are lacking entirely in many areas. Hence, the guerrillas are able to move, undetected, back and forth across the borders to conduct terror operations, to help local Communists to train their own cadres, to indoctrinate the indigenous population, and to fan the dissatisfaction and unrest of the illiterate and backward peoples who inhabit the rural areas of the various nations struggling to maintain stable non-Communist governments.

The government of North Vietnam remains committed ultimately to conquer the entire nation, and guerrilla infiltration has been especially intense in South Vietnam. The terms of the 1954 cease-fire agreements stipulated that all Vietminh forces were to be evacuated to the north. Although approximately 50,000 men were withdrawn from the south, a clandestine hard core remained behind. Moreover, many troops that were removed in 1954 meanwhile have received special training for waging guerrilla warfare and subsequently have been returned to create additional Communist cells, to engage in harassing operations, and to await the signal for overt battle. On occasion, entire battalions have been sent across the border to stir up unrest and to employ terror tactics; other guerrillas have entered indirectly, by way of Laos and Cambodia.

The ruthlessness and intensity of this Communist offensive against South Vietnam increased significantly during 1959 and 1960. On May 4, 1961, U.S. Secretary of State Dean Rusk said that during the past eighteen months the number of armed Vietminh guerrillas operating in that country had grown from about 3,000 to over 12,000. He added:

> This armed strength has been supplemented by an increase in the number of political and propaganda agents in the area.
>
> During 1960 alone, communist armed units and terrorists assassinated or kidnapped over 3,000 local offi-

cials, military personnel and civilians. Their activities took the form of armed attacks against isolated garrisons, attacks on newly-established townships, ambushes on roads and canals, destruction of bridges and well-planned sabotage against public works and communication lines. Because of communist guerrilla activity, 200 elementary schools had to be closed at various times, affecting over 25,000 students and 800 teachers.

This concerted effort by the Vietminh guerrillas to overthrow the non-Communist government of South Vietnam has never diverted their attention from actively assisting indigenous Communists to attain a similar goal in Laos.°
Despite a greater emphasis on subverting South Vietnam and assisting the Laotian Communists to wage a new revolutionary war in their own country, North Vietnamese guerrilla activities in the other adjoining countries of Cambodia and Thailand likewise have been significant. After 1954, the indigenous Communist guerrillas in Cambodia seem to have taken refuge in North Vietnam. Although a clandestine hard core remains in the country, recent guerrilla operations in Cambodia have been directed primarily toward gaining support for the current Vietminh offensive against South Vietnam. Efforts have been made to fan an existing territorial quarrel between the two nations, and some of the infiltration into the south has been carried out via Cambodia. Since April, 1960, when Prince Norodom Sihanouk once more

---

° Developments in Laos, as they evolved between the 1954 cease-fire and mid-May 1961, are discussed in detail on pp. 127–39.

became Chief of State in the reshuffle of power that followed the death of his father, an attempt has been made to align Cambodia more closely with the Communist bloc. Hence, the emphasis now is on exploiting Sihanouk's neutralist tendencies while simultaneously creating as many difficulties as possible for the Western-supported governments of South Vietnam and Thailand, which are the most strongly anti-Communist nations in the area.

In Thailand, infiltration activities have succeeded in establishing a hard core, and agents continue to operate in many areas despite concerted attempts by the government to curb Communist activity. In addition, some Thai have received training in Laos in guerrilla tactics and presumably have returned to their homeland as replacements for some of the agents who have been arrested by the Thai authorities.

So far, no effective way has been found to curb the activities of North Vietnam's clandestine forces. So well have the guerrillas fulfilled their tasks that terror, violence, and a continuing expansion of Communist influence throughout Southeast Asia has to a considerable extent been the result of their operations.

STANDARDIZATION AND MODERNIZATION
OF THE REGULAR ARMY

Despite continuing emphasis on revolutionary guerrilla warfare, since 1954 North Vietnam also has undertaken a variety of measures to improve her regular forces. These efforts have centered around the attainment of five objectives: expanding training activities; modernizing equipment; improving installations and logistics lines; regularizing rank and promotion systems, conscription and demobilization arrangements, salary payments, and uniforms; and intensifying allegiance to Communist ideology.

As a consequence of the drive to improve training, officers' schools have been established and unit exercises have been held more frequently.

There now are training schools for infantry, artillery, and logistics officers. Most are in the capital city of Hanoi, which, of course, is the organizational center of regular army activities. In all these schools, Communist Chinese instructors conduct many of the more advanced courses. Unfortunately, no details are available concerning the numbers of students being trained at the officers' schools, nor do we know very much about their curriculums.

The regular units now hold small-scale maneuvers and combined arms exercises fairly frequently. Since the military forces still consist primarily of infantry units, a number of rifle firing ranges have been set up where target-shooting competitions are conducted as a part of the training program. A few artillery firing ranges also exist, and intensified training gradually has improved the efficiency of the artillery units. In 1958, more complex annual combined maneuvers in which artillery, infantry, engineering, and communications units participate were inaugurated. Although most reports claim that these exercises have helped to improve the capabilities of the troops for combined operations, there has been some criticism from the High Command of performance during these maneuvers. For example, some signal units still seem poorly disciplined. They have refused to participate in maneuvers in bad weather or at night and have failed to maintain their equipment properly.

Although the 1954 armistice terms prohibit the introduction of military aircraft into North Vietnam, liaison and transport aircraft have been furnished by Communist China. Insofar as is known, the Vietminh have not acquired any fighter planes. However, as the recent Soviet airlift of matériel to the Laotian rebels from North Vietnam demonstrated, additional aircraft of whatever type is required can be moved in quickly from either the U.S.S.R. or Communist China. There is strong evidence that some Vietminh pilots are being trained in Communist China, and the curriculums of the various officers' training schools seem to include some courses in the employment of air power. The objective of these aspects of the training program seems to be to prepare the regular forces for a more efficient use of air support in their ground operations and to ready them to cooperate, if necessary, with the Chinese Communists in combined air-ground operations.

A naval training school has been set up at Dang Hai. So far, training has emphasized preparedness for coastal defense. The Vietminh "navy" consists of a few patrol boats and cannot yet serve as an effective attack force.

A methodical program to modernize equipment has been carried out ever since the 1954 cease-fire. At first, the odd assortment of heavier equipment of Japanese, American, French, and other origin with which the Vietminh had fought earlier was being phased out and Chinese equipment phased into the regular units. More recently, the North Vietnamese leaders have become somewhat wary of the growing dependence on China for matériel. On several occasions, they have insisted that non-Chinese equipment be retained. Moreover, some heavier equipment seems to have been obtained from the U.S.S.R.

The Vietminh have done much since 1954 to build up their military installations and logistics lines. Some of the airfields acquired from the French have been improved, and there is evidence that the airport at Lang Son is being prepared to handle jet planes. Development of more effective logistics lines also has included a concerted effort to repair the few railroads and to create better highways, bridges, and roads. It appears that the harbors at Haiphong, Ben Thuy, and Hon Gay, destroyed during the war, have been reconstructed. Emphasis also has been given to establishing a more efficient radio and telegraph communications system. There are unconfirmed reports that forts and fortifications have been constructed at points along the coast where hostile amphibious landings might be expected and that some of the areas suitable for such landings have even been mined. The exact location of these coastal defenses is unknown.

Since the spring of 1958, efforts also have been made to introduce various administrative measures designed to formalize rank, promotion, and salaries. Furthermore, the regular forces have been issued uniforms and insignia, which they are expected to wear when serving on active duty. A series of official regulations issued in May and June, 1958, has served as the legal basis for this drive. However, two factors have delayed the full implementation of the decisions taken at that time. First, the

Ministry of Defense lacks the funds to carry out all its responsibilities simultaneously and has been permitted instead to enforce the new regulations gradually as its budget permits. Second, long-time army personnel who volunteered during the war tend still to prefer the informality of the guerrilla system. Their opposition also has delayed, to some extent, these aspects of the effort to standardize the regular forces.

Other reforms inaugurated in 1958 envisaged the gradual introduction of a more formal system of conscription and demobilization. However, both these measures incited considerable opposition, and as a consequence, the effort to establish a regular system of rotation within the army has proceeded fairly slowly.

Prior to 1958, only ill and injured soldiers had been demobilized, and when able-bodied men were first released from the army, the civilian population, particularly in rural areas, suspected them of disloyalty. The regime, meanwhile, has waged an intensive propaganda campaign to explain the demobilization system to the people, and demobilized soldiers seem now to be more readily accepted into the communities to which they return. Demobilized troops are expected to join the reserve, which was separated from the militia about the same time, as units are organized.

Concurrent with efforts to implement demobilization arrangements, an attempt has been made to establish gradually a nationwide draft system. Experimental compulsory conscription programs have been inaugurated in several pilot centers, including Vinh Phue, Ha Nam, Hai Duong, and Nghe An provinces, the four mountainous districts of Thai Nguyen, and the Phu Yen district of the Thai-Meo Autonomous Zone. Those enlisted have been assigned to duty both in the regular army and in the reserve, and these various experiments have succeeded fairly well. However, particularly in the rural areas where family ties are strong, the people have objected to the idea of having their able-bodied young men drafted into the army when they are needed to work at home. The government, therefore, has seen fit to initiate the draft gradually. A mass propaganda campaign to explain general conscription has been conducted to prepare the population to accept a compulsory universal draft. In a backward country such as North Vietnam, census rolls are either nonexistent or inadequate, and statistical records have to be improved before any meaningful enforcement of universal conscription is practicable.

POLITICAL AND ECONOMIC IMPLICATIONS OF MILITARY REFORMS

Viet military officials have admitted, though sometimes in veiled language, that in addition to strengthening the reserve and enabling rotation in the regular army, the program of gradually inaugurating a universal draft has certain secondary political objectives. One official, Nguyen Van Dien, clearly admitted this in an article in the March 25, 1958, issue of *Quan Doi Nhan Dan* (*The People's Army*):

The application of the military conscription program is not solely aimed at recruiting new soldiers, but mainly at widely publicizing among the people the military policy of the party in order further to raise their patriotism, their sense of national defense, their enlightenment, their hatred for the enemy, and their love for our army, thereby helping them grasp their responsibility, as citizens, to defend the motherland.

Attention to the indoctrination of the troops in Communist ideology has consistently enjoyed highest priority and has been an integral part of all efforts to improve the regular forces.

Ever since the cease-fire, the Vietminh have conducted annual so-called political re-education schools for officers. These courses last several weeks and are devoted solely to instruction in Communist doctrine and strategy. They stress loyalty to the Communist Party and the national leadership, and dedication to all tasks assigned by the Party. Most of them are organized and carried out by the special political commissars attached to the army. Meetings encouraging self-criticism and analysis of past ideological errors follow these formal courses. Similar courses are conducted for enlisted men, to supplement the political indoctrination included in the general military training program. Students at the standard military academies, such as the Artillery Officers' School at Hanoi, also are expected to take courses in Marxism-Leninism specifically tailored to North Vietnam's role in the world Communist movement and to their individual duties and responsibilities as soldiers serving the country's Communist Party.

The series of reform measures promulgated in 1958 included a bill designed to standardize political activities throughout the army; it established the lines of responsibility for political indoctrination and the methods to be applied. Furthermore, the new regulations, by stipulating that Party and government officials *above* the Ministry of Defense were to decide on promotions for the highest-ranking military officers, served to furnish to the Party a formal means of controlling the political loyalty of the entire military establishment. Subsequently, a more intensive drive to increase the effectiveness of political indoctrination was launched by the military leaders. Throughout the years since 1958, political officers and Party members have met frequently at the regiment and division level, as well as at the higher echelons, to plan ways to improve political indoctrination. These efforts have not been entirely successful. Some officers and soldiers still feel that attention should be concentrated on military subjects and exercises and that less time ought to be devoted to politics. In some areas, political indoctrination courses still are poorly planned and halfheartedly conducted.

The 1958 reform measures also envisaged the creation of an enlarged and better-trained reserve as one by-product of the effort to standardize the regular army. Hence, the build-up of the reserves has proceeded concurrently with the various related attempts to increase the efficiency, political consciousness, and viability of the regular forces. Young men who have completed their required service with the regular army now are expected to remain in the reserve after their discharge, as are officers. Reserve officers are obligated to participate in annual training, and yearly retraining exercises gradually are being extended to all enlisted and noncom reservists. Furthermore, those who, for any reason other than poor health, are deferred from the draft in areas where it has been made compulsory also are required to enlist in the reserve. As the number of men between the ages of eighteen and forty-five who are forced to undergo military training grows, it is the younger men who are being drafted into the regular army, while those over twenty-five are incorporated into the reserve. The latter are then classified by age and qualifications as class 1 or class 2 reservists.

Since the effort to establish a reserve separate from the militia began, regular army men, sometimes assisted by militia units, have conducted intensive training programs for the new reserve units. Training methods have varied in the different regions. Some reservists are assembled for a few weeks of intensive training and then returned to their civilian tasks. Others are trained for several weeks at local centers, dividing their time between military training and their regular occupations. Still others, particularly in agricultural areas, have drilled in their spare time after finishing a full day's work in the fields.

As has been the case in the regular army, the reserves are expected to undergo political indoctrination as well as to prepare for military duty, should the need arise. In fact, the current program to build up a reserve serves as a convenient device for readying the reservists for their civilian role in a Communist state. At least as much emphasis is placed on transforming them into loyal Communists ready to help the regime carry out its domestic policies as is given to actual military exercises.

As we have noted, the drive to standardize the regular forces and to establish a reserve has not reduced the role of the guerrillas. In fact, it has freed them for an increase in clandestine operations in nearby countries. Similarly, the various reforms have not nullified the necessity for all members of the armed forces to participate directly in the effort to implement the regime's domestic economic policies. Some of them have even been directed toward increasing the civilian functions of the military units.

The North Vietnamese leaders have met with considerable resistance from the peasants in their attempt to collectivize agriculture and to bring the few factories and mines in the country under the direct control of the state. Furthermore, in the years immediately following the armistice, it was necessary to overcome the peasants' suspicion and fear of all soldiers and to mobilize the masses for the concerted effort to repair war damage and build up the economy.

Between 1954 and 1958, both the regular forces and the militia frequently helped with local civilian projects, such as road-building, irrigation, crop-harvesting, and village improvement. They were a source of emergency assistance to the peasants during floods and other natural calamities. Furthermore, just as during the war, they undertook to indoctrinate the peasants, thereby to increase the ratio of loyalty to the regime within the country as a whole. So-called "soldier-civilian" or "army-worker" projects served the dual purpose of improving the economy and removing some of the suspicions and fears of the peasants concerning the new regime and the army that served it.

The reforms of 1958 included measures to extend the civilian tasks of the army. During that year, some regular units were detailed to establish military collective farms in various regions. Soon it became clear that the regular army was to play an important role in fulfilling North Vietnam's first Three-Year Plan (1958–60). Land reclamation and the establishment of collectives were important points in the Plan. During this period, army units cleared land, planted crops, and acquired livestock. By September, 1959, there were about forty of these army collective farms in various stages of development. Within the Three-Year Plan, all these farms were further built up, new buildings were erected, and personnel were trained to use tractors and improve farming techniques. There are indications that other army units now carry out similar assignments designed to build up the mines and factories of the country.

Army collective farms and the extension of this idea to mines and factories have served several useful purposes. Most important, this increased use of military units to perform civilian tasks has accelerated somewhat the economic development of North Vietnam. Such units remain subject to military discipline and are therefore more efficient than their civilian counterparts. In addition, by making a visible contribution to the country's well-being, the army units assigned to civilian tasks have helped to lessen popular resistance to universal conscription. Moreover, army farms, mines, and factories are providing a means of easing into civilian life those long-time soldiers who are reluctant to leave the army but who have outlived their usefulness to the regular forces because of age or resistance to reform measures and, for one reason or another, are equally unsuited for use in clandestine guerrilla operations. The army, then, still is a most important tool in North Vietnam's continuing effort to socialize and improve the civilian economy.

THE ROLE OF THE VIETMINH IN LAOS

In addition, as events in Laos since the 1954 cease-fire have demonstrated, the Vietminh military establishment, particularly its clandestine guerrilla arm, still is playing an important role in the regime's conduct of its foreign policy. The covert help which the Vietminh guerrillas have furnished to the Pathet Lao in their revolutionary efforts provides a detailed example of how, by working in conjunction with indigenous Communists in surrounding nations, the Vietminh have been able to continue their efforts gradually to complete a regional Communist revolution in Southeast Asia during a period of ostensible peace.

This second revolutionary guerrilla war in Laos was waged by the Pathet Lao from mid-1954 until May, 1961, when once again a cease-fire was declared and the major Western powers, the U.S.S.R., Communist China, and representatives of certain interested smaller nations assembled anew at Geneva with the belligerents to try to negotiate a settlement. As the 1961 Geneva conference on Southeast Asia opened, it still was unclear whether an acceptable agreement could be worked out or whether the Pathet Lao would resume fighting. Irrespective of what the future might bring, the collaboration between the Vietminh and the Pathet Lao since 1954 was an important factor in this second phase of the regional revolutionary war.

Under the terms of the 1954 Geneva cease-fire agreements, the local Laotian Communist dissidents, the Pathet Lao, were to withdraw into the two northern provinces of Phong Saly and Houa Phan (Sam Neua), directly across the border from North Vietnam. They were to remain in armed control there until after elections had been held in 1955. All Vietminh were to be evacuated to North Vietnam, and eventually, the Pathet Lao were to be integrated with the Royal Laotian forces. Neither of these latter objectives ever was realized. Instead, the Pathet Lao, drawing heavily upon Vietminh experience and assistance, applied General Giap's doctrine in conducting a revolutionary guerrilla war of their own.

During 1954 and 1955, the Pathet Lao, with Vietminh assistance, concentrated on building up and training their forces. They emerged sporadically from their base of operations in Phong Saly and Houa Phan to engage in terror operations, sabotage activities, and attempts to expand the pro-Communist cadres in other sectors of the country. Meanwhile, in the coalition government formed after the 1955 elections, a legitimate Communist-front party and its supporters served as an influential minority group, furnishing the Communists some indirect representation in political affairs. In January, 1956, a bona fide Communist Party was created. Soon, as the consequence of an intensive recruitment drive, it, too, was able to set up a well-functioning apparatus operating throughout Laos.

As efforts to build up the military forces continued, the Pathet Lao next undertook lengthy negotiations with Premier Souvanna Phouma on the details of how to integrate their forces with the Royal Laotian Army. Finally, agreements were signed at Vientiane in November, 1957. These provided for the transferring of administrative control over Phong Saly and Houa Phan to the Royal government, the merging of the Pathet Lao with the Royal Army, and the holding of supplementary elections to the National Assembly to permit the Communist Party to compete for seats in that body.

As subsequent events were to prove, the Pathet Lao in 1957 had no real intention of giving up their military independence. Instead, they merely were maneuvering to attain for the Communist Party a legitimate place in a coalition government and the concomitant right to exercise direct influence over governmental decisions. An important objective was to control the flow of Western foreign aid to the Royal government. In the coalition cabinet formed on November 18, 1957, Prince Souphanouvong, the political leader of the Pathet Lao, became head of the ministry responsible for negotiating all foreign-aid agreements.

As implementation of the coalition agreements signed at Vientiane proceeded, the behavior of the Communists foreshadowed the crisis that was to occur. There was no opposition to the installation of Royal governors in the two northern provinces, which remained their military stronghold. However, the Pathet Lao did take steps to ensure the continued autonomy of their guerrilla forces. Kayson Phomvihane, one of their military leaders, went underground in the bush with a hard core. Some Pathet Lao guerrillas took temporary sanctuary across the border in North Vietnam; most other units, although now formally a part of the Royal Army or its reserves, remained in the two northern provinces, kept their own officers, and continued to operate as semi-independent forces. In ostensible acceptance of the Vientiane agreements, North Vietnam temporarily withdrew those of its guerrilla cadres identifiable as such, along with some equipment.

During this period, Premier Souvanna Phouma succeeded in disbanding the tripartite International Supervisory and Control Commission, which, since 1954, had been supposed to police the adherence of the Laotian belligerents to the terms of the cease-fire. Actually, it had been completely ineffective; now it adjourned *sine die*, and its members returned to their respective countries of Poland, India, and Canada.

The scheduled supplementary elections to the National Assembly were held in May, 1958, and the fact that the Communist Party made a strong showing may have alerted those anti-Communist factions that all along had opposed coalition. In any event, Souvanna Phouma's coalition government fell late in July, 1958, and in August a strongly anti-Communist regime took charge, with Phoui Sananikone as Premier.

Despite the new government's efforts to suppress the Communists, guerrilla activities and internal unrest continued. Guerrilla terror operations increased once more, and supplies and men were reinfiltrated across the border from North Vietnam. Since a proposed agreement to define more clearly the poorly demarcated boundary between the two countries never had been ratified during the brief period of "peaceful coexistence," infiltration remained as difficult to prove as ever.

Throughout 1959, the situation deteriorated. During January and February, a dispute flared up over a North Vietnamese charge of border violations by Royal Laotian troops in the vicinity of Houng Lap village. By May, the continuing skirmishes in the north had begun to be accompanied by some military activity further south. For example, a Pathet Lao unit on the Plaine des Jarres that ostensibly now was a part of the Royal Army refused to participate in an integration ceremony. Though encircled and pursued, it succeeded in gaining sanctuary across the North Vietnamese border. As military skirmishes continued, particularly in the north, Prince Souphanouvong was arrested by the Royal government.

During this period of increased unrest, a few regular North Vietnamese troops occasionally participated in operations in the northern regions, but that country's assistance to the Pathet Lao consisted primarily of serving as a sanctuary and a source of matériel and guerrillas so ethnically similar to the Pathet Lao fighters that it was virtually impossible to prove their identity. Hence, the fact-finding commission sent by the United Nations in response to an appeal by Laos early in September for an "emergency force" to stop what it termed "flagrant aggression" on the part of North Vietnam did not find sufficient justification for U.N. intervention. And, of course, the U.S.S.R. vigorously opposed such a move. However, in its report of November 6, 1959, to the Security Council the U.N. investigatory group did indicate that North Vietnam had furnished equipment, arms, supplies, and the help of "political cadres" to the Pathet Lao.

The behavior of the Communist guerrillas during 1959 was completely true to their doctrine: Neither military nor political developments had reached the stage where the time was ripe to launch a counteroffensive. Hence, the Pathet Lao avoided pitched battles, emphasized instead all other means of wearing down the enemy, and retreated when necessary.

The year 1960 brought a new upsurge of military skirmishes incited by the Pathet Lao, and the Royal government, split by this time into even more factions struggling for power among themselves, proved totally unable to form a stable regime. Premier Phoui Sananikone had resigned on the last day of 1959, and a military junta under General Phoumi Nosavan had taken over. Elections to a new National Assembly were held late in April, 1960, with such a sweeping majority for the right-wing non-Communist candidates that the elections did not accurately reflect the rapid growth of the Communist Party throughout the country.

The capability of the government to maintain authority did not improve. On May 24, Prince Souphanouvong escaped from prison with fifteen followers, apparently to return to the Communist military stronghold in the north. Captain Kong Le was responsible for another *coup* on August 9. On September 2, he reinstated Souvanna Phouma as Premier, and together they embarked on a policy of ending "the killing of Lao by Lao." The Soviet Union was invited to open an embassy in the country, and pledges of friendly relations with Communist China and North Vietnam were issued. Perhaps Souvanna Phouma and Kong Le sincerely were trying to strike a balance between pro-Communism and the strongly anti-Communist policies of the government they had overthrown, thereby establishing a truly neutral regime. If so, the Communists soon succeeded in manipulating them for their own purposes so that they no longer retained the freedom of action essential to implementing a bona fide policy of neutrality.

After Souvanna Phouma's intentions to expand relations with the Communist bloc became apparent, a new crisis arose. General Phoumi Nosavan withdrew his former allegiance to Phouma and set up a separate headquarters for those Royal troops he controlled at Savannkhet, in southern Laos. Soon, Nosavan's forces had taken over the Royal capital of Luang Prabang.

By December, 1960, the two factions of the former Royal Army—one loyal to Kong Le and Premier Souvanna Phouma, the other to General Nosavan—were fighting each other for control of the administrative capital of Vientiane. The King refused to take sides. Meanwhile, the Pathet Lao forces were intensifying their activities to stir up unrest in other areas. On December 9, when it appeared that General Nosavan's forces would succeed in taking Vientiane, Premier Souvanna Phouma fled to Cambodia. Soon, Soviet planes landed at the Vientiane airport with howitzers and ammunition for the Kong Le forces. Eventually, General Nosavan won the artillery duel and

installed Premier Boun Oum as head of the Royal government. Meanwhile, airdrops of Soviet matériel from
bases in North Vietnam to the Pathet Lao had been inaugurated, and the Communist forces had emerged from
their northern stronghold to wage a war of movement
in the Plaine des Jarres, where Kong Le's troops also were
battling those parts of the Royal Army still loyal to
Nosavan, and therefore to the pro-Western regime he had
set up under Boun Oum.

Late in December, 1960, and early in January, 1961,
the Boun Oum government once more appealed to the
United Nations for help, but it later admitted that it
deliberately had exaggerated the extent of assistance of
North Vietnam to the Pathet Lao when it reported to the
U.N. that seven battalions of troops had entered Laos
from North Vietnam. The actual number of North Vietnamese guerrillas fighting with the Pathet Lao was never
clearly determined, but it is safe to assume that the Pathet
Lao received whatever supplementary manpower they
deemed necessary.

As the crisis deepened, it gradually became apparent
that the Communists were applying a somewhat different
strategy, both locally and at the international political
level, from the one they had employed when the Vietminh,
late in 1953, had launched their counteroffensive in the
earlier war against the French. This time, Prince Souvanna
Phouma and Kong Le's forces were being utilized by the
Communists as a "temporary ally." The Pathet Lao formed
a military coalition with the anti-Western Kong Le forces
and concentrated on defeating the main enemy: the pro-
Western forces of General Nosavan. Moscow and the

entire Communist bloc issued pious proclamations recognizing Souvanna Phouma as the "rightful ruler of Laos," thereby seeming to side against the local Communists and with those nations who advocated a neutral government for Laos.

Working out a way to deal with this crisis posed a particular dilemma for the free world. The United States continued its program of military assistance, which provided that the U.S. furnish matériel, funds, and instructors to the Royal government, after the Boun Oum regime came to power.* However, during the first months of 1961, as the fighting went on and the rebels gained more territory, it became increasingly clear that U.S. military assistance alone would not save Laos. France, preoccupied with other problems in Algeria and elsewhere and disgruntled by the anti-French policies of the Boun Oum government, was reluctant to become any more deeply involved. Great Britain favored negotiation. The SEATO powers feared that any action on their part might incite expansion of the conflict. India, Cambodia, and other Asian nations proposed various measures for a cease-fire and a negotiated settlement.

President Kennedy, in a policy statement on March 23, 1961, publicly made clear the United States position. He said in a press conference that although the United States favored constructive negotiation among the nations concerned and the establishment of a truly neutral govern-

---

* During the 1954 cease-fire conference at Geneva, the U.S. had refrained from signing the final treaty. Hence, the U.S. assistance program, unlike the help furnished to the Laotian rebels by the Vietminh, by the U.S.S.R., and perhaps by Communist China, violated no international agreements to which the United States was a signatory.

ment in Laos, "there first must be a cessation of the present armed attacks by externally supported Communists."

The Communists remained deliberately ambiguous about whether they would honor the U.S. proviso that its presence at the conference table was contingent upon a prior cessation of rebel military activities, and the fighting continued. However, preparations to convene a fourteen-nation conference, with the Foreign Ministers of the U.S.S.R. and Great Britain serving as co-chairmen, already were under way. It was agreed that the other nations to participate would be Burma, Cambodia, Canada, Communist China, France, India, Laos, North Vietnam, Poland, South Vietnam, Thailand, and the United States. After many delays, much confusion, and new diplomatic tangles, some of the delegations were assembling at Geneva by May 11. The U.S. accepted a somewhat dubious last-minute assurance by members of the reactivated tripartite International Supervisory and Control Commission that a cease-fire had taken place in Laos, but for almost five days, procedural problems delayed the opening of the Geneva negotiations and caused a considerable number of new difficulties for the West. The Soviet Union insisted that all three of the dissident Laotian factions be seated on an equal basis. The United States argued that the Pathet Lao could not claim full governmental status and opposed granting the Pathet Lao the same standing as that of the Boun Oum regime. Finally, the U.S. agreed to admit the Pathet Lao on an equal basis. Then the Boun Oum regime's delegation, objecting to this compromise, said it would refuse to attend the opening session. The conference finally opened on May 16, 1961, without any representatives of the Royal Laotian government in attendance. The delegations from two other strongly pro-Western Southeast Asian nations that were scheduled to participate, South Vietnam and Thailand, had not yet arrived, although they were reported to be en route. To add to the confusion, negotiations between representatives of the rebel military coalition and General Nosavan's Royal troops in Laos itself were beginning to create new problems. Although the two rival military groups had met for the purpose of discussing procedural details of maintaining the cease-fire, the Pathet Lao immediately had insisted that this group proceed at once to work out a plan for a coalition government for Laos.

Whatever the future might bring, one thing was certain: The struggle of the Pathet Lao eventually to complete a Communist revolution in Laos by one means or another would continue indefinitely. Once again, by careful timing and co-ordination of local military and political operations with pertinent international developments, the Communists had maximized their opportunities for a settlement at Geneva that was bound to be more favorable to them than to the West. Furthermore, if events required, the "temporary alliance" with Souvanna Phouma and Kong Le could be severed without notice, and the Pathet Lao could resume independent fighting free from the encumbrances imposed by a coalition policy at any time they chose. While the Pathet Lao had not abandoned their objective of completing a Communist revolution in their country eventually, the specific tactics they would utilize in the future and the extent to which assistance from the Vietminh would continue would be governed by actual developments in the real world. Although the Communists claim for themselves an ability to predict the future course of history, their policies always are based on retaining sufficient flexibility of action to compromise when necessary in order to gain an opportunity to advance more vigorously at a later date.

This second Communist revolutionary war in Southeast Asia, in Laos, as it had evolved between mid-1954 and mid-May 1961, had been carried out under far easier conditions than those the Vietminh had faced during their own earlier overt struggle against the French. The Pathet Lao's opponent was an indigenous group, split into several factions and subfactions and therefore highly susceptible to Communist maneuvers to break down enemy unity and morale. This enabled the Communists to enter into a temporary coalition with one of these factions and concentrate, for the moment, on trying to defeat the pro-Western element within the non-Communist camp. The Vietminh had helped to train and build up the Pathet Lao's guerrilla forces, had furnished supplies and ammunition, and had assisted in terror operations. Furthermore, the Pathet Lao had been able to seek temporary sanctuary across the border in North Vietnam as events required. The Laotian war also had served to emphasize the current importance of the Vietminh guerrillas as the arm of North Vietnam's military establishment best suited for operations in surrounding countries. So far, Vietminh guerrilla operations have succeeded so well that waging this regional revolutionary war has not even required

North Vietnam to utilize her regular troops to carry out a full-scale invasion of a neighboring country.

❖   ❖   ❖

From this review of developments since the cease-fire, it is clear that the Vietminh military establishment is succeeding in adapting its organization and policies to the current and future role it is expected to play. Since 1954, it has become an increasingly essential instrument of the regime's effort to realize its foreign and domestic goals.

The story of military developments in North Vietnam since the 1954 cease-fire is an account of slow but steady progress. The Vietminh are building a regular army equal in readiness and strength to that of the strongest Southeast Asian non-Communist nations. Simultaneously, the covert guerrilla arm of the Ministry of Defense is being utilized to subvert surrounding nations and to prepare them for a Communist revolution. Furthermore, North Vietnam is continuing effectively to utilize its military personnel at home to help build up and industrialize a backward economy and to develop a society completely loyal to the Communist regime, to its policies, and to the revolutionary objectives of Communism per se.

VII

CONCLUSIONS

This study has addressed itself primarily to the military aspects of the war in Indochina. However, in Vietminh theory—as in all Communist theory and practice—political and military aims are intertwined and inseparable, with the political objective taking precedence over the military at all times. If necessary, a short-term military advantage has always been sacrificed to political gain. Consequently, the Communists in Indochina did not draw clear distinctions among the various available means by which to achieve their ultimate objective of domination. In contrast to Western practice, they did not create specialists. Their conception of the soldier's function and training was basically different from ours, and the difference was mainly a doctrinal one, even though the shortage of manpower made it a practical necessity as well. Each soldier had to be not only a fighter, but a propagandist, a political agent, and even a laborer, as the situation required.

In countries where the Communists have become the established power, their armies tend to follow our own trend toward greater professionalization and specialization. In underdeveloped and as yet unconquered areas that call for guerrilla tactics, however, the need for the versatility and flexibility of the soldier-propagandist-laborer will no doubt always exist. One of the lessons of the war in Indochina is that, in training troops that may have to face guerrilla-type warfare, the West would do well to broaden its own concept of military duty to include a larger variety of ways in which each soldier must be prepared to serve.

FUNCTION AND IMPORTANCE OF THE GUERRILLA

While the Communist doctrine of revolutionary war posits as its final goal the creation of a modern army in the Western sense of the word, Vietminh revolutionaries—theorists as well as practitioners—from the very beginning recognized the crucial value of the guerrilla in the underdeveloped country and difficult terrain in which they were operating. Their idea of the guerrilla fighter and their refinement of guerrilla warfare beyond any point in previous historical experience go far toward explaining their ultimate success.

The precedent of Indochina, with its important lesson on the potential value of the guerrilla in all phases of revolutionary war, is not likely to have been lost on the Communist bloc. Moreover, the Korean experience has shown that an attack in force may invite American intervention, a possibility that any future Communist plan for usurpation will want to avoid as far as possible. Even though Communist-bloc countries may be increasingly able to put regular forces into the field, it is conceivable that they will find guerrilla warfare a safer and more attractive alternative in underdeveloped areas. This approach would have all the advantages that were proved in Indochina: slow attrition of the local enemy, relative safety from countermeasures, time in which to build up regular forces for the decisive final attack, and cheapness. It would also create serious problems for the United States, which not only lacks forces trained and equipped to fight a low-level guerrilla war but, moreover, would not be able morally to justify intervention. The Communists might well speculate, therefore, that the United States would consider intervening only in the final, overt phase of a war, by which time the position of the defending side would be bad, perhaps even hopeless. At the time of Dien Bien Phu, for example, the United States decided against intervention largely for that reason.

The novelty and much of the strength of the Vietminh's approach lay in a broad and sophisticated conception of the guerrilla army and its functions. A French officer defined the Viet idea of guerrilla warfare as "the totality of action undertaken against the rear of the enemy in order to weaken his material and moral strength and reduce his freedom of action." Certainly, the Viet guerrillas were no small, roving bands of men with improvised tasks. They were a trained force—although not in the sense in which the term is applied to the regular army—with specific and detailed missions, as important to psychological warfare as to the military operations that were conducted in Indochina. His realization of the primacy of political penetration and conquest was indeed one of the keys to Giap's success. In his view, the natives had to be won for the revolutionary cause to the point not merely of acquiescence but of active participation in the struggle. The means to this end included an understanding of their political preconceptions and their social customs, of their needs and aspirations, that only intimate knowledge and a keen intelligence network can supply. It was essential, furthermore, to break down the instinctive, traditional barriers of distrust between citizenry and army, and to make a visible effort to furnish economic aid (a primary need in all underdeveloped countries). In the attainment of these objectives, the value of guerrillas was clearly inestimable. In Indochina, they were able to perform the feats of infiltration that gave the Vietminh their advantage of superior intelligence; they aided in vital nonmilitary tasks—such as harvesting, emergency relief, and public improvements—that earned them the gratitude of the natives; and their "irregular" status and frequent practice of not wearing uniforms helped overcome the sense of separation and suspicion that easily prevails between civilians and regular soldiery.

From the military point of view, guerrilla tactics, with their heavy reliance on mobility, were obviously what the terrain and the military situation in Indochina demanded, and many of the principles of guerrilla warfare—rapid movements (preferably at night), massive but brief attacks on the battlefield, quick disengagement from actions with doubtful prospects—were applied also to the operations of the regular army. The success of Vietminh guerrilla tactics in restricting the movements of the French along the few available roads, in cutting their land and water lines of communication, and in forcing them to take to the air (where they were limited in the extent and effectiveness of their operations by the number of aircraft and airfields) may well have created a precedent for future Communist ventures in countries whose physical and political properties resemble those of Indochina.

The case of Indochina also demonstrates the crucial role of a powerful friendly neighbor who can provide material, technical, and moral assistance to the revolutionaries. Here again, the siege of Dien Bien Phu, which highlighted the Communist success, provides a good illustration. Without the Vietminh victory at Dien Bien Phu, and its political repercussions, the war would probably not have ended when it did but might have dragged on for years. A siege-like battle on the scale of Dien Bien Phu, with its heavy requirement for artillery and manpower, would have been unthinkable without the constant supply line from Communist China and without the ease of access of personnel from one country to the other. Not for many years, if ever, could the Vietminh alone have manufactured the artillery necessary for the decisive battle against the French, and it needed the experience and expertise of the Chinese to train the Vietminh soldiery and military leadership, both in China and in Vietnam. In both respects, the advantage of contiguity was vital: Without a common border, the logistic problem of moving men and weapons would have been formidable so long as the French controlled both sea and air. There can be no doubt whatever that China's interest in supporting the revolutionaries, coupled with the common border, was a strong contributing—if not the decisive—factor in the success of the Vietminh.

WEAKNESSES OF REVOLUTIONARY WARFARE

The Vietminh campaign demonstrated some of the weaknesses of revolutionary warfare as well as its advantages. Particularly during the early war years, the Viet effort suffered considerably from poor logistics, shortages of money and matériel, lack of trained officer cadres, and hence an inability to carry out sustained attacks. The very primitiveness of techniques and equipment helped to render some of these weaknesses less serious than they might have been for an army of greater complexity. The lack of hard cash with which to pay for imported weapons became an incentive for local production of a surprisingly large output of matériel of a simple kind, and soldiers as well as forced laborers were chiefly paid in kind, and very little at that. Lack of a modern transportation system, and the concomitant need for staggering numbers of coolies, often created a shortage of manpower, which would have been far more severe, however, if the war needs had called for transport of POL and of large amounts of artillery ammunition, and if those primitive means of transport had not had the incidental advantage of being virtually immune to conventional means of detection and destruction. The poor logistic system did, as we have said, reduce the Vietminh's capacity for sustained operations. Also, preparation for an attack required the prestocking of supplies in the battle area, which sometimes did not escape detection and thus gave away the plan. Lack of modern weapons and the chronic manpower shortage combined, furthermore, to reduce the need for formal military training, for the Vietminh could not afford the luxury of the kind of specialization found in modern armies. The resultant shortage of high-echelon officers to be placed in command of large-scale operations, and of skilled technicians who might have hastened the development of the artillery and the engineering corps, remained Giap's particular concern and unquestionably lowered the combat efficiency of his army. This handicap was partly compensated for by the fanatic dedication of the existing officer cadres and by the centralization of control in the hands of the top leaders. The high degree of centralization, which has sometimes been criticized as a general Communist failing, was thus in fact dictated by the special circumstances of the Indochinese war.

ADVANTAGES OF THE REVOLUTIONARIES

Some of the advantages of the Vietminh over the French were inescapable. The infiltrating techniques of the Viet guerrillas and their greater familiarity with country, terrain, and people placed at their disposal a fund of intelligence material that the French could not hope to equal. Racial characteristics that rendered native Viet fighters indistinguishable from peaceful inhabitants of the villages provided perfect camouflage, whereas the French reconnaissance elements, by their dissimilarity, were easy targets and had no way of "merging" with the population. The absence of fronts, as we know them, and hence of a rear that could be regarded as safe from enemy action, compelled the French to protect every installation individually and thus tie up many thousands of troops in local security. The scarcity of so-called strategic targets and the profusion and elusiveness of tactical targets made target acquisition an almost hopelessly difficult task for the French air force. And photo reconnaissance, so important to Western armies, was hampered by heavy vegetation, mountainous terrain, and frequent bad weather. Furthermore, the French were slow to develop counter-tactics to the Vietminh's effective use of such devices as direct fire with camouflaged artillery pieces, which the revolutionaries substituted for the more conventional indirect massed artillery fire. It took the French a long time to understand Vietminh guerrilla ambush methods and to develop countermeasures. In short, they essentially failed to realize, until late in the war, that their principal military encounters were with the guerrilla element of the Vietminh forces, against which the conventional tactics of Western armies were inapplicable.

Some Lessons for the Future

The pattern as it has evolved in Indochina since the beginning of the war is typical of the Communists' present-day methods of hiding behind and exploiting indigenous "national-revolutionary" movements; only *after* Ho's regime had come to power in North Vietnam did it openly admit its ties with the Communist bloc. The same trend is apparent today in other parts of Southeast Asia and even in Latin America.* The experience of Indochina

---

* See *Che Guevara on Guerrilla Warfare* (New York: Frederick A. Praeger, 1961).

permits several generalizations about Communist principles and methods that are likely to hold true for many
of these vulnerable areas. Understanding them should
help the United States in planning how to deal most effectively with guerrilla operations and politico-military unrest in small or underdeveloped countries.

To begin with, Moscow and Peking have much to gain
from confining themselves to the covert and proxy military
support of local guerrillas and national revolutionaries
during what Giap has termed the first two stages of the
protracted conflict. Even in the third and final stage,
there are distinct advantages in limiting such outside
assistance to covert training and shipments of matériel.
Having the local cadres seemingly take the initiative and
carry the Communist struggle to its conclusion minimizes
the risks of direct Western intervention, through the
U.N. or otherwise. More important, it virtually deprives
the West of any justification for introducing nuclear
weapons into the conflict and for directing diplomatic or
military retaliation against Moscow and Peking.

In Indochina, the main advantage of Giap's strategy
over that of his opponents proved to be flexibility of
action. Attempts to win popular support through friendly
actions, for example, were combined with terror, and even
the concept of the protracted conflict in three stages was
singularly elastic. The successful experience of the Vietminh in merging military with nonmilitary forms of conflict and in keeping their strategic concepts and tactical
practices highly flexible could be applied in future situations. Furthermore, with the necessary modifications, the
principles and methods that brought the Communists to

power in North Vietnam are as well suited to preparation for a *coup d'état* as they are to a lengthy war of attrition.

The advantages that accrued to the Vietminh from their conception of the soldier as a man of multiple functions—psychopolitical and civil as well as military—have been described in some detail. We have also mentioned their reasons for maintaining close control from the center over all command decisions and activities until a trained army had been created. It is well to bear in mind that in most areas of Africa, with their low literacy level and lack of trained leaders and specialists, the Vietminh organizational experience would be particularly applicable.

The Western powers now have granted independence to most of their former colonies in Asia, Africa, and Latin America and, in most instances, have withdrawn their troops. Whatever foreign troops remain stationed in these areas can act only at the request of the national sovereign. This situation greatly enhances the Communists' chances of avoiding a protracted conflict, with its risky "third phase" of open warfare. Rather, they may aim to exploit factionalism among local nationalist leaders and military groups in order to bring about a *coup d'état* at the appropriate moment. Our own planning should be geared to the very real possibility that in the future, Vietminh philosophy and tactics will be applied, with modifications, in Communist exploitation of local unrest. Wherever the political and military elites of an underdeveloped nation have been successfully infiltrated and an indigenous hard core built up with outside assistance and guidance, a relatively slight intensification of guerrilla operations at the right moment could conceivably bring a Communist regime to power very quickly. Overt invasion by conventional troops, with its attendant risks, would thus become unnecessary. Moreover, should the attempt at a sudden *coup* fail, the involvement of outside forces would be extremely difficult to trace. This hypothetical development is a considerable change from the situation in Indochina, where the Vietminh had to cope with a foreign government essentially impervious to infiltration and was forced to fight the well-trained and adequately equipped French troops. Today, despite various alliance commitments— SEATO, CENTO, etc.—the major Western powers are unlikely to risk central war in order to prevent a seemingly indigenous Communist group from staging a *coup*. Intervention by the United Nations might be difficult to justify, since the Communists would take pains to stress the "internal" nature of the conflict.

In conclusion, it is well to bear in mind that, while advances in technology are introducing new weapons at a rapidly increasing rate, these do not render obsolete all of the more primitive forms of military conflict, nor do they detract from the importance of guerrilla warfare. In our planning and in our military training programs, we must be prepared for all contingencies, and much can be learned from the military and psychopolitical problems that France encountered in Indochina.

EPILOGUE*

The Vietnamese Communists—the Viet Cong—are clearly embarked on a strategy very similar to the one they pursued in the war against the French. Although Vietnam today is an independent republic headed by an elected president, Ngo Dinh Diem, Communist propaganda continues to play up the colonialist issue by denouncing Diem as a pawn of American imperialists and trying to convince the Vietnamese that, in casting off French rule and becoming a republic under American domination, they merely exchanged one colonial master for another. Needless to say, the massive U.S. economic and military assistance program, and the physical presence of many Americans in Saigon—planned as they are to support Diem in his struggle against Communism—are grist to the Red propaganda mill. Communism, according to the Viet Cong line, is not only the solution to the country's social and economic problems but the one road to true independence.

To judge by the observable evidence of their tactics, the Viet Cong have accepted the idea of the protracted war, with its long and patient build-up toward victory,

* In June–July, 1961, after this book had gone to press, the author had the opportunity to revisit South Vietnam and to check his earlier conclusions against observations made during this trip. These findings are summarized in the pages that follow.

151

and are not thinking of an immediate and violent seizure of power. However, if they were in fact planning in terms of a *coup d'état*, their present efforts and preparations would also prove most useful to that end by providing an excellent basis for a new Communist government.

In reality, at least as far as the Communists are concerned, the earlier war has never ended. With the armistice and the subsequent proclamation of the Vietnamese Republic, the Communists in the south merely went underground, and the struggle for total conquest of Vietnam has continued ever since, directed and aided by the government of North Vietnam.

Perhaps the most patent and persuasive form of outside assistance is the program of daily broadcasts by Radio Hanoi, beamed not only at the Vietnamese elements but also at the minority mountain tribes (known as *montagnards*) along the Laotian and Cambodian borders. With the latter, the propaganda line is simple and direct: Playing on the *montagnards'* fear and dislike of the Vietnamese, it asserts that Diem is planning to take over "their" country and otherwise prejudices them against the legitimate government. Moreover, Radio Hanoi broadcasts music that the *montagnards* like, and thus has become a favorite station with these people, whose lives hold few pleasures and little recreation. In its broadcasts to the Vietnamese population, Hanoi exploits the continuing respect for Ho Chi Minh, whose statements carry considerable weight, for he is still considered a great nationalist even by many non-Communist Vietnamese. Apart from these direct appeals, North Vietnam furnishes guidance for propaganda originating in South Vietnam and supplies the personnel to help conduct it. Some of these experts are South Vietnamese who were taken to the north in 1954 for political training and have since been returned in order to aid the Communist struggle in the south.

In their efforts to win popular support, the Viet Cong are employing the familiar combination of persuasion and terror so successful in the past. Pamphlets, tracts, and magazines from the north are distributed widely, even in some of the cities that are firmly under government control. Viet Cong agents make it a practice to go to the villages, where the inhabitants are compelled to assemble and listen to their propaganda speeches. Probably the most effective method is to implant rumors and Communist philosophy in an individual and allow him to spread them by word of mouth. This is a favorite technique for disseminating reports about the strength of the Viet Cong, circulating lies about American domination and exploitation in South Vietnam, and exaggerating incidents of misbehavior by the Vietnamese army against local civilians. Though the success of these methods cannot be gauged accurately, they are having considerable impact. There are entire areas in South Vietnam that are definitely friendly to the Communists and actively hostile to the government and its officials.

The organized rebel forces flaunt their own flag and have an official organization for political action—the Committee for the Liberation of South Vietnam. Despite frequent rumors that the Communists intend to establish a rival government within South Vietnam, they have not thus far attempted to do so, possibly because they do not yet have a secure point of control and base of operations (though in Communist doctrine this would not necessarily be an insurmountable handicap).

For the present, military action, and even paramilitary activities, are being subordinated to the struggle for political conquest, and there have been few formal troop engagements. Notwithstanding the attacks by several hundred Viet Cong in the autumn of 1960 and again before the elections in April, and the more recent battle east of Saigon in July, 1961, in which hundreds of troops of both sides were involved, the general strategy has been to concentrate on guerrilla and terrorist action.

The dual goal of these low-level activities is to paralyze and emasculate the present regime and to create a vacuum in the lower echelons of government. In pursuit of the first objective, the rebels have been using their old tactic, the ambush, in order to inhibit travel on the roads and canals of South Vietnam. This tactic is highly effective in a country that, in spite of steady improvements, still has relatively few roads and only one railroad. As a result, it is becoming more difficult for government officials to collect taxes, dangerous for the peasant to take his produce to market, and impossible, or at least hazardous, in some sections for the central government to maintain the degree of contact necessary if it is to make its will felt in areas outside the capital. Even army units are finding it slow and risky to move about.

In the closely related effort to cause chaos among the lower officialdom of the Diem government, the Viet Cong seem to be concentrating their terrorist attacks especially on village and district chiefs, who have become the targets for assassination or abduction, and whose families are subjected to often savage reprisals for the officials' independence or opposition. This has created an enormous problem for the central government: On the one hand, it is clearly impossible to provide a bodyguard for every provincial official; on the other hand, these men will have to be protected if the Viet Cong are to be prevented from systematically wiping them out and thereby cutting off an indispensable administrative link between Saigon and the outlying districts.

A recent and flagrant example of this tactic demonstrates how far the Viet Cong are prepared to go, particularly if they find their own objectives undermined by a successful governmental action for the general welfare. With help from the United States, the Diem government has undertaken a malaria-control program, but the Viet Cong have recently tried to jeopardize the effort by attacking and killing the agents who are being sent out into the country to help train the local authorities in fighting this most serious health hazard.

The bases and training camps of the Viet Cong have been established in remote jungle and mountain areas of the country, where they are virtually immune to detection and access. Here the men are carefully indoctrinated in Communist ideas and are trained in guerrilla warfare as well as in the elementary tactics of companies and, possibly, battalions. Forces that are now being employed for guerrilla and terror operations will ultimately become the nuclei of larger, formal units if the Communists continue to operate on the theory of the protracted, three-stage conflict.

The problem of supplies, however, continues to trouble

the Viet Cong. Indications are that they lack a single major supply line that could bring in massive quantities of matériel and arms from the north. The so-called Ho Chi Minh Trail is no more than a series of paths that run north and south through the mountains and are not suitable for large arms shipments. Conceivably, the Communists are receiving some heavy supplies by way of sampans and junks that take the sea route from North Vietnam and land secretly in the south. By the most reliable estimates, however, this system is not being used extensively. To judge by equipment and arms that have been captured from the Communists, they have been fighting largely with home-made weapons and with such matériel of French and American make as they have been able to steal or capture. Indeed, some observers maintain that entire Viet Cong operations are planned with the primary mission of capturing equipment from the Vietnamese army.

North Vietnam's greatest contribution, at present, lies in furnishing guidance, moral support, trained cadres, and perhaps a limited amount of specialized equipment.

The impressions the writer gained during his recent visit to South Vietnam fully confirm his earlier conclusion that the Communists in Indochina are continuing their strategy of deliberate political action supported by only as much military activity as they consider necessary in order to advance their cause. One major change, however, has occurred in the situation. Washington today is far more aware than formerly of the nature and extent of the threat to South Vietnam, and is prepared and preparing to meet it. And the U.S. government's growing understanding of Communist goals and methods is reflected in Saigon, where American officials, even at this late hour, are trying to help stem the tide of Communist successes.

However, the crucial fact today is that the Communists are arousing the people to fight and work for them. It is easy but wrong to attribute their success solely to terrorist methods. They are systematically creating the "sea" that Mao thought essential for military success and eventual political control. Diem has been unable to win popular support either on a nationalist basis or with personal loyalty as a motivating force. Until his government has the active and continuing support of the Vietnamese masses and the troops, all the economic and military aid in the world, though it may delay it, will not halt the Communist advance.

SELECTED BIBLIOGRAPHY

Many of the French materials that constitute the basis for this book cannot be cited at this time and therefore are not included in the bibliography.

BOOKS AND PAMPHLETS

BARTHOUET, A. *Le Livre du vétéran: les psychoses de guerre.* Paris, 1952.

BLANCHET, ANDRÉ. *Au Pays des ballila jaunes: relation d'un correspondant de guerre en Indochine.* Paris, 1947.

CATROUX, GENERAL. *Deux actes du drame indochinois.* Paris, 1959.

CHASSIN, GENERAL L. M. *Aviation Indochine.* Paris, 1954.

Che Guevara on Guerrilla Warfare. With an Introduction by Major Harries-Clichy Peterson. New York, 1961.

CHÉZAL, GUY DE. *Parachute en Indochine.* Paris, 1947.

CRÈVECOEUR, COLONEL DE. *Aperçus sur la stratégie du Viêt-Minh.* Paris, 1953. [Mimeographed.]

———. *Raccourci de la campagne d'Indochine (depuis 1945 à 1950).* Paris, 1952. [Mimeographed.]

DELPEY, ROGER. *Glas et Tocsin.* Paris, 1952.

———. *Nam-Ky.* Paris, 1951.

———. *Parias de la gloire.* Paris, 1953.

———. *Soldats de la boue.* Paris, 1950.

DEVILLERS, PHILLIPPE. *Histoire du Viêt-Nam 1940–1952.* Paris, n.d.

DINFREVILLE, J. *L'Opération Indochine.* Paris, 1953.

FALL, BERNARD B. *Street Without Joy.* Harrisburg, Pa., 1961.

———. *The Viet Minh Regime.* New York and Ithaca, N.Y., 1954. [Issued jointly by the Institute of Pacific Relations and the Southeast Asia Program, Cornell University.]

——. *Le Viet Minh, 1945–1960.* Paris, 1960.

GOELDHIEUX, CLAUDE. *Quinze mois prisonnier chez les Viêts.* Paris, 1953.

GRONIER, M. *Riz et pruneaux—avec les commandos dans la brousse Indochine.* Paris, 1951.

GUILLAIN, R. *La fin des illusions: notes d'Indochine.* Paris, 1954.

HAMMER, ELLEN J. *Struggle for Indo-China.* Stanford, Cal., 1954.

JENSEN, FRITZ. *Erlebtes Vietnam.* Berlin, 1955.

KILLIAN, R. *Les fusilliers marins en Indochine.* Paris, 1948.

LACHEROY, COLONEL CHARLES. *Action Viêt-Minh et communiste en Indochine ou une leçon de "guerre révolutionnaire."* Paris, 1955. [Mimeographed.]

——. *Une armée du Viêt-Minh: les hiérarchies parallèles.* Paris, 1954. [Mimeographed.]

——. *Scénario-type de guerre révolutionnaire.* Paris, 1955. [Mimeographed.]

LEWIS, NORMAN. *A Dragon Apparent: Travels in Indochina.* London, 1951.

MAO TSE-TUNG. *Strategic Problems of China's Revolutionary War.* Peking, 1954.

——. *On the Protracted War.* Peking, 1960.

MARCHAND, GENERAL JEAN. *Le drame Indo-Chine.* Paris, 1953.

——. *Indo-Chine.* Paris, 1949.

——. *L'Indochine en guerre.* Paris, n.d.

MORDAL, JACQUES. *Marine Indochine.* Paris, 1953.

MUS, PAUL. *Viêt-Nam: Sociologie d'une guerre.* Paris, 1952.

NAVARRE, GENERAL HENRI. *Agonie de l'Indochine.* Paris, 1957.

NAVILLE, P. *La guerre du Viêt-Nam.* Paris, 1949.

NEMO, COLONEL. *En Indochine: Guérilla et Contre-Guérilla.* Paris, 1952. [Mimeographed.]

NEWMAN, BERNARD. *Report on Indo-China.* London, 1953.

NGO VAN CHIEU. *Journal d'un combattant viêtminh.* Paris, 1955.

NGUYEN, DUY THANH. *My Four Years with Viet Minh.* Bombay, 1950.

PAGNEZ, YVONNE. *Français d'Indochine.* Paris, 1953.

——. *Le Viet Minh et la guerre psychologique.* Paris, 1955.

PIREY, PHILIPPE DE. *Operation Waste: Parachutists in Indo-China.* London, 1954.

READ-COLLINS, N. *Report on War in Indochina.* London, 1953.

RENALD, JEAN. *L'Enfer de Dien Bien Phu*. Paris, 1955.

RENAUD, JEAN, and ONG-CHÚA. *Ho Chi Minh, Abd-El-Krem et Cie*. Paris, 1949.

RIESEN, RENÉ. *Jungle Mission*. London, 1957.

ROY, JULES. *La bataille dans la Rizière*. Paris, n.d.

SABATTIER. *Le destin d'Indochine*. Paris, 1952.

SAINTENAY, J. *Histoire d'une paix manquée*. Paris, 1953.

STAROBIN, JOSEPH. *Viet-Nam Fights for Freedom*. London, 1953.

U.S. DEPARTMENT OF STATE, OFFICE OF PUBLIC AFFAIRS. *Indo-China: The War in Southeast Asia*. Washington, D.C., 1951. [Mimeographed.]

VALÉRIE, ANDRÉ. *Ici, Ventilateur*. Paris, n. d.

VO NGUYÊN GIAP. *La guerre de libération et l'armée populaire*. [Hanoi], 1950.

PERIODICALS AND BULLETINS

BALDWIN, HANSON W. "A Hell of a Place to Have to Fight in," *Life* (March 31, 1961).

CHASSIN, GENERAL L. M. "Guerre en Indochine," *Revue de Défense Nationale* (July, 1953).

———. "Lessons of the War in Indochina," *Interavia*, VII, No. 12, 1952.

CHERNE, LEO. "Deepening Red Shadow Over Vietnam," *The New York Times Magazine* (April 9, 1961).

COUSINS, NORMAN. "Report from Laos," *Saturday Review* (February 18, 1961).

CROCKER, LIEUTENANT COLONEL H. E. "Indo-China—An Appreciation," *Army Quarterly* (April, 1953).

DRISCOLL, COLONEL J. J. "The Indo-China War—A French Dilemma," *Air Force Magazine* (January, 1953).

DUCKWORTH, FLIGHT LIEUTENANT J. W. "The Portent in Southeast Asia: The Fate of Indo-China," *Air Power* (January, 1956).

DURDIN, PEGGY. "The Shadowy Leader of the Viet Minh," *The New York Times Magazine* (May 9, 1954).

———. "The Grim Lesson of Laos," *The New York Times Magazine* (May 21, 1961).

ENNIS, T. E. "Operation 'Survival' in Laos," *Current History* (March, 1961).

FALL, BERNARD B. "Indo-China—The Seven-Year Dilemma," *Military Review* (October, 1953).

——. "Indo-China—The Last Year of the War: Communist Organization and Tactics," *Military Review* (October, 1956).

——. "Indo-China—The Last Year of the War: The Navarre Plan," *Military Review* (December, 1956).

——. "The Laos Tangle," *International Journal* (Spring, 1961).

FITCH, LIEUTENANT COLONEL M. "The RCAMG in Indo-China," *Canadian Army Journal* (January, 1956).

HOGARD, J. "Guerre Révolutionnaire et Pacification," *Revue Militaire d'Information* (January, 1957).

"Indochine '53." Supplement to *Forces Aériennes Françaises*, No. 87 (April, 1953).

JONAS, ANNE M., and TANHAM, GEORGE K. "Laos: A Phase in Cyclic Regional Revolution," *Orbis* (Spring, 1961).

KOCH, CAPTAIN H. G. "Terrain Tailors Tactics in Indochina," *Army Combat Forces Journal* (April, 1954).

"Laos and the Communists' New Dream of Conquest," *U.S. News & World Report* (January 16, 1961).

LINEBARGER, MAJOR P. M. A. "Indochina—The Bleeding War," *Army Combat Forces Journal* (March, 1951).

McGEE, SENATOR GALE W. "Vietnam: A Living Example for Implementing the American Spirit" [address to U.S. Senate, February 9, 1960], in *Vital Speeches of the Day* (May I, 1960).

MALGONKAR, MAJOR M. D. "The Situation in Indo-China," *Military Review* (June, 1952).

MARTIN, H. "Guérilla, Guerre en Surface, Guerre Révolutionnaire," *Revue Militaire d'Information* (August, 1957).

MARTIN, LIEUTENANT COLONEL N. E. "Dien Bien Phu and the Future of Airborne Operations," *Military Review* (June, 1956).

MARTIN, R. P. "At the 'Front' in Laos: An Eyewitness Report," *U.S. News & World Report* (January 23, 1961).

O'BALLANCE, MAJOR EDGAR. "Dien Bien Phu," *USI of India Journal* (April–June, 1956).

PAUKER, G. J. "The Future of Vietnam," *Foreign Policy Bulletin* (November 1, 1956).

PRESTAT, CAPTAIN. "La Guerre psychologique en Indochine: ses opérations et ses résultats." [Text of a lecture, delivered on

September 14, 1955, in a course on psychological warfare given at Boblingen. Mimeographed.]

PROSSER, MAJOR LAMAR F. "The Bloody Lessons of Indochina," *Army Combat Forces Journal* (June, 1955).

Revue Militaire d'Information (February–March, 1957). [Entire issue devoted to revolutionary war.]

RIGG, LIEUTENANT COLONEL ROBERT B. "Red Parallel: Tactics of Ho and Mao," *Army Combat Forces Journal* (January, 1955).

"SEATO Council Representatives Consider Situation in Laos," *The Department of State Bulletin* (January 23, 1961).

SOUSTELLE, JACQUES. "Indo-China and Korea: One Front," *Foreign Affairs* (October, 1950).

STEINER, H. A. "Viet-Nam: Civil War Again?" *The New Republic* (July 18, 1955).

"Terrorism in Vietnam," *America* (April 23, 1960).

TOPPING, SEYMOUR. "India on the Razor's Edge," *Foreign Affairs* (April, 1951).

"U.S. Cites Evidence of Soviet and North Vietnamese Aid to Lao Rebels," *The Department of State Bulletin* (January 23, 1961).

"United States Expresses Concern over Situation in Laos," *The Department of State Bulletin* (August 24, 1959).

"U.S. Refutes Soviet Statement on American Position in Laos," *The Department of State Bulletin* (September 7, 1959).

"The United States White Paper on Laos, January 7, 1960," *Current History* (March, 1961).

"Vietnam's Gains Spur Red Terror," *Business Week* (July 18, 1959).

WARNER, D. "Borders Are Dissolved," *The New Republic* (November 28, 1960).

———. "Indo-China: Have We Learned the Lessons of the War?" *The New Republic* (December 14, 1959).

"Where Reds Are Trying to Grab Another Country," *U.S. News & World Report* (May 2, 1960).

WRIGHT, P. "Laos: Wrong Place for a War," *The Reporter* (February 16, 1961).

OTHER VOLUMES OF RAND RESEARCH

THE UNIVERSITY OF CHICAGO PRESS, CHICAGO, ILLINOIS

Water Supply: Economics, Technology, and Policy, by Jack Hirshleifer, James C. DeHaven, and Jerome W. Milliman, 1960

COLUMBIA UNIVERSITY PRESS, NEW YORK, NEW YORK

Soviet National Income and Product, 1940-48, by Abram Bergson and Hans Heymann, Jr., 1954
Soviet National Income and Product in 1928, by Oleg Hoeffding, 1954
Labor Productivity in Soviet and American Industry, by Walter Galenson, 1955

THE FREE PRESS, GLENCOE, ILLINOIS

Psychosis and Civilization, by Herbert Goldhamer and Andrew W. Marshall, 1953
Soviet Military Doctrine, by Raymond L. Garthoff, 1953
A Study of Bolshevism, by Nathan Leites, 1953
Ritual of Liquidation: The Case of the Moscow Trials, by Nathan Leites and Elsa Bernaut, 1954
Two Studies in Soviet Controls: Communism and the Russian Peasant, and Moscow in Crisis, by Herbert S. Dinerstein and Leon Gouré, 1955
A Million Random Digits with 100,000 Normal Deviates, by The RAND Corporation, 1955

HARVARD UNIVERSITY PRESS, CAMBRIDGE, MASSACHUSETTS

Smolensk under Soviet Rule, by Merle Fainsod, 1958
The Economics of Defense in the Nuclear Age, by Charles J. Hitch and Roland McKean, 1960
The Real National Income of Soviet Russia Since 1928, by Abram Bergson, 1961

THE MACMILLAN COMPANY, NEW YORK, NEW YORK

China Crosses the Yalu: The Decision To Enter the Korean War, by Allen S. Whiting, 1960
The Determination of Orbits, by A. D. Dubyago; translated from the Russian by R. D. Burke, G. Gordon, L. N. Rowell, and F. T. Smith, 1961
Protective Construction in a Nuclear Age, edited by J. J. O'Sullivan, 1961

McGRAW-HILL BOOK COMPANY, INC., NEW YORK, NEW YORK

The Operational Code of the Politburo, by Nathan Leites, 1951
Air War and Emotional Stress: Psychological Studies of Bombing and Civilian Defense, by Irving L. Janis, 1951
Soviet Attitudes toward Authority: An Interdisciplinary Approach to Problems of Soviet Character, by Margaret Mead, 1951
Mobilizing Resources for War: The Economic Alternatives, by Tibor Scitovsky, Edward Shaw, and Lorie Tarshis, 1951
The Organizational Weapon: A Study of Bolshevik Strategy and Tactics, by Philip Selznick, 1952
Introduction to the Theory of Games, by J. C. C. McKinsey, 1952
Weight-Strength Analysis of Aircraft Structures, by F. R. Shanley, 1952
The Compleat Strategyst: Being a Primer on the Theory of Games of Strategy, by J. D. Williams, 1954
Linear Programming and Economic Analysis, by Robert Dorfman, Paul A. Samuelson, and Robert M. Solow, 1958
Introduction to Matrix Analysis, by Richard Bellman, 1960
The Theory of Linear Economic Models, by David Gale, 1960

THE MICROCARD FOUNDATION, MADISON, WISCONSIN

The First Six Million Prime Numbers, by C. L. Baker and F. J. Gruenberger, 1959

NORTH-HOLLAND PUBLISHING COMPANY, AMSTERDAM, HOLLAND

A Time Series Analysis of Interindustry Demands, by Kenneth J. Arrow and Marvin Hoffenberg, 1959

FREDERICK A. PRAEGER, NEW YORK, NEW YORK

War and the Soviet Union: Nuclear Weapons and the Revolution in Soviet Military and Political Thinking, by H. S. Dinerstein, 1959
Divided Berlin: The Anatomy of Soviet Political Blackmail, by Hans Speier, 1961

PRINCETON UNIVERSITY PRESS, PRINCETON, NEW JERSEY

Approximations for Digital Computers, by Cecil Hastings, Jr., 1955
International Communication and Political Opinion: A Guide to the Literature, by Bruce Lannes Smith and Chitra M. Smith, 1956
Dynamic Programming, by Richard Bellman, 1957
The Berlin Blockade: A Study in Cold War Politics, by W. Phillips Davison, 1958
The French Economy and the State, by Warren C. Baum, 1958
Strategy in the Missile Age, by Bernard Brodie, 1959
Foreign Aid: Theory and Practice in Southern Asia, by Charles Wolf, Jr., 1960
Adaptive Control Processes: A Guided Tour, by Richard Bellman, 1961

PRENTICE-HALL, INC., ENGLEWOOD CLIFFS, NEW JERSEY

Games of Strategy: Theory and Applications, by Melvin Dresher, 1961
Information Processing Language-V Manual, edited by Allen Newell, 1961

PUBLIC AFFAIRS PRESS, WASHINGTON, D. C.

The Rise of Khrushchev, by Myron Rush, 1958
Behind the Sputniks: A Survey of Soviet Space Science, by F. J. Krieger, 1958

RANDOM HOUSE, INC., NEW YORK, NEW YORK

Space Handbook: Astronautics and Its Applications, by Robert W. Buchheim and the Staff of The RAND Corporation, 1959

ROW, PETERSON AND COMPANY, EVANSTON, ILLINOIS

German Rearmament and Atomic War: The Views of German Military and Political Leaders, by Hans Speier, 1957
West German Leadership and Foreign Policy, edited by Hans Speier and W. Phillips Davison, 1957
The House Without Windows: France Selects a President, by Constantin Melnik and Nathan Leites, 1958
Propaganda Analysis: A Study of Inferences Made from Nazi Propaganda in World War II, by Alexander L. George, 1959

STANFORD UNIVERSITY PRESS, STANFORD, CALIFORNIA

Strategic Surrender: The Politics of Victory and Defeat, by Paul Kecskemeti, 1958
On the Game of Politics in France, by Nathan Leites, 1959
Atomic Energy in the Soviet Union, by Arnold Kramish, 1959
Marxism in Southeast Asia: A Study of Four Countries, edited by Frank N. Trager, 1959
The Unexpected Revolution: Social Forces in the Hungarian Uprising, by Paul Kecskemeti, 1961

JOHN WILEY & SONS, INC., NEW YORK, NEW YORK

Efficiency in Government through Systems Analysis: With Emphasis on Water Resource Development, by Roland N. McKean, 1958